WRITE MORE GOOD

An Absolutely Phony Guide

THE BUREAU CHIEFS

THREE RIVERS PRESS
NEW YORK

Published in the United States by Three Rivers Press, an imprint of the Crown Publishing Group, a division of Random House, Inc., New York.

www.crownpublishing.com

Library of Congress Cataloging-in-Publication Data

Bureau Chiefs.
Write more good : an absolutely phony guide / The Bureau Chiefs.—1st ed.
1. Mass media—Humor. 2. Satire, American. 3. Journalism—Style manuals—Humor. I. Title.
PN6231.M33B87 2011
818'.602—dc22 2010042088

ISBN 978-0-307-71958-4
eISBN 978-0-307-71959-1

Printed in the United States of America

Book design by Maria Elias
Illustrations by Benjamin Birdie
Cover design by Kyle Kolker
Cover photography © istockphoto/Zoran Kolundzija

10 9 8 7 6 5 4 3 2 1

First Edition

The Bureau Chiefs would like to thank:
Keith Andress and David Larsen, our legal eagles;
Kate McKean and Stephanie Chan, without
whose guidance we would be lost;
and most of all our friends, family, and loved ones,
who put up with this crap long before we
convinced the world to pay for it.

The Bureau Chiefs would also like to thank
the Bureau Chiefs.
Those guys are hilarious.

CONTENTS

A FANCY FOREWORD BY ROGER EBERT

At Chicago's old City News Bureau, a training ground from the Front Page Era, a motto was on the wall behind the desk of A. A. Dornfeld, the legendary editor and mentor to thousands, such as Kurt Vonnegut and Mike Royko:

"If your mother says she loves you, check it out."

In the minds of many newspapermen, if they will be honest, another motto is engraved:

"Never check a great quote twice."

The authors of *Write More Good* exist in the no-man's-land between these two quotes. They know about Dornfeld's rule. They also give voice to the deep cynicism and cheerfully ironic worldview that has infected city rooms since time immemorial.

My friend McHugh, who once worked the overnight shift at the *Chicago Daily News*, took pride in inspiring a barroom fight at least once a week.

The phone would ring, and a drunk would want the paper to settle an argument.

"What do you say?" McHugh would ask. He would listen, nod, and say, "You are absolutely right. Now put your friend on."

Then he would tell the friend the same thing.

But there's more than cynicism in the observations of @FakeAPStylebook, this book's progenitor.

There is truth from hard-learned experience: "Avoid Top Ten lists, as it just encourages readers to write in with their own additions as if we care about their opinions."

There is knowledge from long experience: "While it is acceptable to include a politician's office address in a profile, do not list their ManHunt user ID."

There is prudence: "When plagiarizing, be sure to use the word 'reportedly.'"

There is realism: "There is no apostrophe in 'Diners Club' but who cares? What is this, 1953?"

Although @FakeAPStylebook is ideal as a Twitter stream and has reputedly reportedly gathered more followers than Justin Bieber, I would like to praise the authors for not doing what anyone else in the Internet age would have done, which is simply cutting and pasting together a slew of tweets, calling it a book, and raking in the dough from old media.

No, these journalists, for they deserve the honorable title, have gone to all the trouble of *actually writing a book*. Within their souls lurks the dream of every newsroom hack: One of these days, he's gonna take off a few months and write something good. What you will find within the pages of this book (reported by many to be alarmingly brilliant and a timeless masterpiece) is intelligence. These are not cub reporters, still less some kid trying to write while his mom is bugging him to come up to dinner.

As one who has worked professionally on newspapers since before he was old enough to get his driving license (note: this usage sidesteps the old "driver's" versus "drivers'" license controversy), I can tell you these people have paid their dues, know the business, and have a clear view of the hypocrisy and pandering that go on in all media, new and old. They also have a veteran newsperson's contempt for authority figures.

About the authors of @FakeAPStylebook I know nothing. Reportedly, allegedly, however, they include A. A. Dornfeld himself, now 109, and Royko, whose notes from the 1970s have been lightly rewritten. Sources who wish to remain anonymous tell me that Perez Hilton, after a long stretch of writing his column, unwinds by violating two or three stylebook rules before calling it a day. The upstairs neighbor of one of the authors says he was always a quiet, well-mannered man who didn't bother anybody. The mother of another says, "This isn't the way my boy was raised."

WriTE
MoRe
gOOd
wRItE
MOre
GOoD

<1>

NEWS

& HEADLINE WRITING

& YOU

& JOURNALISM

YOUR HARD WORK

What's black and white and red all over? The latest victim of the Convent Slayer. And people will be reading about his crimes in YOUR NEWSPAPER!

Welcome to the exciting world of newspaper journalism! Since you're looking to write for a newspaper, it's safe to assume you haven't read one recently, but don't let those stories scare you—newspapers are just as important now as when they were first banged out on clay tablets to announce strikes by the pyramid builders' union. A shifting market and model has always been the lot of the good ol' newspaper industry.

Much has changed since the heyday of the newspapers in the forties and fifties. In the twenty-first century the reporter with his press card–adorned fedora and notepad has given way to a guy in a laser-etched bubble helmet holding a Venusian calculotron. One used to have to wait weeks to be outraged that Dorothy Lamour was smoking around her newborn baby and feeding it martinis, but now every celebrity mini scandal can be shrieked immediately to a spellbound audience. In addition, unlike in the forties and fifties, everybody knows that Clark Kent is Superman. But for both an old-school journalist with a manual typewriter and a modern one with a BlackBerry, one rule remains the same: Do NOT drop that sucker in the bathtub.

THE BASICS

A glance at any front page will tell you that the foundation of journalism isn't great writing. Hell, it's not even good writing. **Finely honed reporting skills** are much more valuable to your everyday journalist-about-town. Think of yourself as a plumber, sniffing out problems and making a huge stink until you've rooted it all out. The only difference is that you'll do your plumbing with a pen, not a pipe wrench. Oh, and unlike a plumber fixing a sewer pipe, nobody's going to pay you forty-six dollars an hour when a story breaks at three a.m.

When trudging through the fetid slush of everyday life in order to pick out the most interesting nuggets and polish them into something vaguely useful, your number one tool will be **the ability to develop sources**.

If you're one of those old-school journalists who strive to maintain credibility, you're going to want to cite authoritative sources in your story. Sources are your readers' only guarantee that you haven't simply invented the news out of whole cloth, like *Toronto Baconburner* reporter Seamus P. McHoserknocker did for three years straight from 1967 to 1981.

After all, if a source said it, you probably can't get sued for reporting it.*

Every journalist should see the movie *All the President's Men*. (There was a book, too, but with the movie you can enjoy the outrageously dated clothes and hairstyles.) Once

*The Bureau Chiefs take no responsibility for lawsuits resulting from the application of this rule of thumb.

you've seen this film, which dramatizes how two intrepid reporters revealed presidential corruption and helped bring down an administration, you'll have an appreciation for how ridiculously easy your job is. Those suckers had to actually investigate stories, while all you do is **touch up the latest press release from the White House**. Sure, the current president may be doing things that would make Nixon's hair curl, but hey, you're getting a paycheck.

#

The **"who, what, where, why, when"** model for writing news stories is based on the principle that these questions are the most important ones a reader would have. "*Who* is responsible for the torsos floating in the river? *What* are they using to kill those women? *Where* along the river are they dumping the bodies? *Why* do I get these headaches and black out whenever I see a dirty whore? *When* will this torment end?"

#

Whether you're calling on the phone or physically going somewhere to do reporting, you should always **identify yourself as a reporter**. Do this by shouting, "I am a reporter!" at the top of your lungs every few minutes, even if someone else is talking.

#

No matter your beat, you will often be called on to attend **news conferences**. Please be courteous to other print and television reporters at these events by shouting your unanswered requests for the speaker's attention at the same volume as them. If you do manage to get called on for a question, always ignore what the speaker said in his or her opening remarks and ask about a hot issue he or she knows nothing about, something he or she said five years ago, or a gerbil-based sex scandal.

#

Newspapers often employ entire departments of **fact-checkers and correction writers**. Do your part to stimulate the economy and keep these hardworking kill-joys employed by inserting blatantly false information into your stories, keeping track of which ones make it through to see how gullible your readers are. Our personal best was an obituary for Charles Nelson Reilly detailing how he and Eva Braun committed suicide in a bunker during the final days of World War II.

#

Reporters place a high premium on **the confidentiality of their sources**. The promise of anonymity can make recalcitrant informants feel freer to open up when discussing issues that may compromise their safety or careers. There is, however, no legal right for a journalist to keep a source confidential, as many reporters have learned after a forty-eight-hour stint in the county lockup for contempt of court. The only known exception to this rule is Father Dervlin O'Maloney, of the Catholic *Daily Free Press* of Newark, who conducts all his interviews in the form of a confession.

Therefore, when informing a source that his statements will be "off the record," keep your index and middle fingers crossed and hidden behind your back.

Alternatively, use controlled substances. But don't use cheap by-the-gallon hooch; spring for the good stuff if you want the story to pay off. (If the source is a politician, replace "hooch" with "Colombian blow" or "beautiful Thai ladyboys.")

#

Plagiarism is the second-worst sin you can commit as a journalist, after inaccuracy. Take your cue from Edward

R. Murrow, who is an inspiration to all journalists everywhere. Holy shit, could that dude drink.

#

Pundits predicting **the death of published newspapers** are displaying their ignorance of simple biology. Since newspapers are protective shells excreted by *Mary Worth* comics, their existence is a part of nature. And believe us, if there's any species that is immune to extinction, it's *Mary Worth*.

#

Having trouble finding an audience for your **food section**? Consider running a story similar to the "mad cow disease scare," e.g., "irritable chicken syndrome," "moody pork disorder," or "uncomfortably needy fish situation." Remember, vegetables do not have feelings.

#

Do not use emoticons in headlines or the body of your text. If for some reason your story is about actual emoticons, please kill yourself.

#

Follow the guidelines on **successfully segmenting a story** over multiple pages. Your readership will appreciate the cohesion of—*cont. on page 334 of this book.*

QUOTING

Quote accuracy may be scalable in the interest of assigning work time to where it does the most good:

When quoting the president of the United States, make damned sure you've got it correct down to the punctuation and pauses. You don't want to get "disappeared," do you?

When quoting a showbiz celebrity, "close enough" is usually good enough, unless said celebrity is known for lawyering up at the drop of a hat. Even when a complaint arises out of a misquote, that's usually good for a few more articles and corrections mentioning the celebrity's name: a win-win publicity situation for all concerned.

When quoting for a "person on the street" piece, just make the quotes up. Christ, it's hot out there this year.

Always use full names and, when possible, occupations and cities of residence when quoting a source for a story. This is largely so that the lawyers of those you write about know who is to blame.

KEEPING IT LOCAL

Every budding journalist dreams of becoming the next Woodward, Bernstein, or (if he or she prefers hallucinogens to concise writing) Hunter S. Thompson. But for the overwhelming majority, the reality will turn out to be a long, thankless stint of wage slavery at the offices of some small-market local paper.

Local papers are often praised as bastions of community-based journalism that address the issues directly impacting their readers (stories that would otherwise be ignored by those hoity-toity city folk at the national dailies). After spending six hours watching the city council furiously debate the appropriate color for the concession stand at the high school football field, however, one tends to suspect that the folks at the national papers may have the right idea after all.

Writing for a local paper requires certain skills:

- Resisting the urge to kill the copy editor/owner's son when he adds a misspelled Comic Sans headline to your article on a fatal traffic accident.
- Avoiding the temptation to add "He looks forward to bagging your groceries after graduation" to a family-commissioned profile of the high school's star quarterback.
- Living with the terrifying knowledge that you live in a town populated by aliens who have learned to communicate by listening to political talk radio, if the letters to the editor are anything to go by.
- Accepting the fact that four years of racking up student loan debt at Columbia resulted in having to write six-hundred-word articles about an octogenarian pan flute player who smells like cat pee.

PERSONAL ADS

Sure, we could have put a vaguely humorous guide here with jokes like how "SWF" means something like "Skanky Weezer Fan" or something, but the truth is, most newspaper personals are more sad than sexy these days. All of the real freaks have gone online, where they can seek out their specific sexual quirk on "asthmasluts.com" or "The Bisquik Enema Chatroom." That leaves only pathetic, pure-vanilla cold cases to place normal ads.

There is one lucrative demographic still interested in the personals, though: murderers! Since half the people calling up on a given day will be seeking victims to kill and devour, it's probably worth it to consider combining your paper's ad sales division with the crime beat to improve operating efficiency.

YOUR ONLINE READER

The Internet has redefined not only how the news is reported but also how newspaper reporters interact with their readers. Thanks to the miracle of online message boards and comment boxes, readers can thoughtfully respond with their analysis of reported events. Alternatively, they can mash the keyboard with their greasy hands until something resembling human language appears on the screen. Here's what you should know about these readers:

- They always have numbers in their online "handles" to distinguish themselves from the other ninety-five "steelersfans" or "luvprincesses" out there.
- Whether their pet project is trying to prove that the mayor is a "libral terrist" or announcing that hemp will save us all, every single story you publish will somehow tie in to it.
- You will be reminded of the many details and trivial asides you "forgot" to mention in your story. Try not to punch your monitor when reading these.
- They are definitive proof against the existence of a benevolent God.

Before responding to comments, ask yourself these questions:

- Will this accomplish anything fruitful?
- Could this message merely be a cat walking across an unattended laptop?
- Has my Facebook feed updated lately?

CRIME WRITING

If movies have taught us anything, it's that crime reporters are hard-nosed, jaded veterans who bring down gangsters and corrupt politicians. Essentially, they're the Batmans of the journalism world. Keep in mind that the crime beat requires cultivating a set of difficult skills, like remaining detached from the horrors encountered on the job and being able to choose between the foxy key witness and the buxom court reporter.

When arriving at a crime scene, it is imperative **not to disturb or touch anything** that could be considered evidence; doing so will both jeopardize the police investigation and make you part of the story. This includes items such as doorknobs, furniture, various weapons you see lying around, dead bodies, living bodies, the floor, the air around you, your own clothes, your pen, and your notepad. If you just can't stop yourself from grabbing a couple bites out of the open bag of Cheetos in the corner of the room, at least ask someone first.

#

In the course of your reporting, odds are you'll be called on at some point to **interview the members of a grieving family** following a crime or other tragedy. Always be sensitive to their feelings and avoid exacerbating their sorrow by following these tips:

- Start with basic, less troubling questions, like "How do you feel?" or "What will you remember most about your loved one?" before moving on to the important ones, like "Approximately how long was his head in the trash compactor?"

- Under no circumstances should you grab your tie and hold it up as if it were a noose or describe working on deadline as "murder."

- Save phrases such as "those poor bastards" for the car ride home with the photographer.

- Laugh uproariously at the bereaved's jokes, even though they will almost certainly not be funny and may not even sound like jokes.

- The phrase "it could have been worse" may not be as comforting as you think.

- As much as you may want to hug them, don't. A few quick, firm pats on the upper thigh are more than enough.

#

Police officials and corporate spokespeople may—and probably will—refuse to answer your calls or give comments for your stories. In such cases it is appropriate to use subtle threats like "I'll tell" or minor rewards like "I'll be your friend" to get them to talk. If they still refuse to go on the record, you may write that the source "declined to comment on the basis of being a big mean ol' booger-eating meanie."

JOURNALIST BACKUP CAREER WORD MATCH!

Journalism may be a dying art, but fortunately that means journalists are uniquely suited to pursue other dead occupations as backup careers. Match the famous journalists with their heretofore unknown safety jobs!

1. Helen Thomas
2. Anderson Cooper
3. George Will
4. Christopher Hitchens
5. Jane Bryant Quinn
6. Charles Krauthammer
7. Paul Krugman

a. snuffbox factory manager
b. Ogham translator
c. viola da gamba player
d. Victorian hair locket crafter
e. jean jacket bedazzler
f. Beanie Baby investments counselor
g. Foghat groupie

ANSWERS: See our Teacher's Edition

HEADLINE WRITING

Like composing haiku or playing Windows Solitaire, writing headlines is a craft that takes even the best copy editors a lifetime to master. A good headline condenses the story into a short, easily grasped phrase without resorting to cheap gimmickry or undue cleverness. A great headline, however, is all about cheap gimmickry and undue cleverness.

The headline is your first, best, and only chance to grab the attention of potential readers. You don't want to bore them to death with accuracy, originality, or clearnessizing.

Use small words, go for the cheap laugh, and don't be afraid to utterly contradict the story. After all, Rupert Murdoch might be reading, and you'll be needing a job when this rag goes belly up in eighteen months, tops.

EXAMPLES

1. **NO:** MLK Blvd. renovation meeting draws SRO crowd
   YES: Black Monday: Race riots overrun city hall

2. **NO:** Sen. Hicks indicted in blackmail scandal
   YES: HIX HOX SEX PIX

3. **NO:** House torpedoes health-care bill
   YES: Fuck you, Tiny Tim!

4. **NO:** Senior citizens petition Congress for expanded prescription benefits
   YES: Drug gang threatens politicians

5. **NO:** Chihuahua has puppies
   YES: Sharp increase in Mexican immigrant population

6. **NO:** Happy babies play in pool
   YES: Splash: Gays in public water sports display

When composing a headline, the most crucial task is to **convey the necessary information** as briefly as possible while remaining vague enough that people will actually read the article. LEGISLATORS DOOM AMERICA is a good example of this approach; WHAT ARE THOSE CLOWNS IN WASHINGTON DOING NOW? is less effective.

A hint of sex appeal can also be useful for this. TOPLESS WOMAN CAUSES STIR is more enticing than TORSO FOUND IN RIVER.

Avoid using abbreviations in headlines. Although space is at a premium and brevity is important, clarity is even more vital. NO-SHOW PREZ IN VET MED SCAN may fit nicely above the fold, but it is more than slightly misleading for a story about the head of the Northern Showjumpers Association unveiling a new X-ray device approved for use on horses.

People make fun of that DEWEY DEFEATS TRUMAN headline, but you know what? They still talk about it. And how many other headlines from that day can you name? Well, apart from TRUMAN DEFEATS DEWEY.

AN IMPORTANT NOTE ABOUT SEXIST LANGUAGE

Back in the good old days, when men could smoke and drink in their offices and sexually harass their secretaries on a daily basis without fear of repercussions, no one had to worry about "inclusive language." Men did all the important work, so the masculine pronoun was just assumed in sentences where gender wasn't specified in the antecedent. That's just the way things were.

Now, with women holding half of all management, professional, and related occupations in the United

States, they've taken on more and more responsibilities. Among other things, this has really screwed up the English language.

None of the options people have come up with, like "shim," "zie," or "hershey" (and "he/she," which has only a narrowly applicable use within the world of transgender porn), have satisfactorily caught on.

So it's up to you to find some solution that will make your writing nonsexist in order to appease all the PC whiners while also avoiding pronoun-antecedent agreement errors. Here are some options:

> SEXIST: Everyone pees standing up unless he has to shit as well.
>
> INCORRECT: Everyone pees standing up unless they have to shit as well.
>
> CORRECT: Everyone pees standing up unless he or she has to shit as well.
>
> ALSO CORRECT: People pee standing up unless they have to shit as well.

GLOSSARY

Associated Press Stylebook Some bullshit. Thinks it's important, but it's not.

attribute Cite the original source of a quote you "edited."

banner A headline that extends across the width of a page. Important: DO NOT MAKE IT ANGRY.

beat 1. The news subject on which someone reports, e.g., crime beat, sports beat. 2. When one news outlet gets a story before another. 3. What the editors do to reporters who get 2-ed on their 1.

bias Viewpoint or perspective reflecting a personal opinion or attitude. Unrelated, but isn't this book the greatest thing in the world? Also, Yankees suck. Go Sox!

Bias, Len Boston Celtics draft pick who died from an overdose in 1986 . . . or so the liberal media would have you believe.

blind interview You expected a Stevie Wonder joke, didn't you? Go elsewhere for your crude humor, sir, you'll find nothing of the sort here! Good day!

blogosphere Proof that an infinite number of monkeys in front of an infinite number of computers will eventually type up spoilers for next week's episode of *Doctor Who*.

breaking news Phrase used to signify the most urgent of developing events, such as a nuclear meltdown, a fender bender in IKEA's parking lot, or a missing kickball at a local elementary school.

burying the lede Originally a reference to the disappearance of Ledish gangster Gunnar "The Lede" Magnusson, who was allegedly buried under an ice hockey rink in Stockholm.

bylines Currency newspapers use to pay reporters.

caption Text accompanying a photo or illustration to explain its contents. That's a real definition, look it up! Now you can charge this book as a business expense!

Chicago Manual of Style Some people use this as their grammar and usage guide. Some people also fuck sheep. What's your point?

circulation The sound of uncontrollable sobbing.

clarification Short blurb showing that a story wasn't really wrong, but some picky asshole wanted to split hairs.

clippings Clean them up. Didn't your mother teach you better?

column A regular feature in a newspaper written by that guy down the hall who plays Farm Town and naps all day.

correction Short blurb admitting your story was "wrong" because some picky asshole wanted to split hairs.

coupons The Sunday paper's main selling point; consider running your most important stories in this section.

cut When a certain copy editor named Tim arbitrarily removes sentences from your well-written story to make the copy fit in the column and because he is a douche.

dateline Telephone line for lonely reporters and correspondents on assignment. Because sometimes you just need someone to hold you in this crazy industry.

deadline Something reporters say they're on so they don't have to talk to you on the phone.

exclusive Print journalism: a story that only one news source has. TV journalism: any news story.

fedora Traditional headgear of old-time reporters. Wear

one today and you're not just a guy with a hat, you're That Guy with the Hat. Don't be That Guy.

folo Slang for "follow-up story," i.e., the same story you ran yesterday with two paragraphs of new information.

font A basin of water used in religious rites, particularly blessings. Also, another word for typefaces. There's probably some reason this one word means two totally different things, but since we flunked out of English and became journalism majors, we don't know it.

Fourth Estate A term journalists use to make themselves feel like they make important contributions to society so they don't eat a gun after covering their twentieth ham-and-beans fund-raiser.

freelancer A reporter without health insurance.

funnies Antiquated term for a newspaper's section of comic strips, many of which were, at one time, humorous. Now primarily of interest for *B.C.*'s occasional anti-Islamic screeds. Consider replacing with a new term, like "the groanies."

gutter White space between columns of print or pages. Also, where we usually wake up on Sunday morning covered in vomit, coupons, and glitter.

hard news Live or current news that usually goes on the front page. Not to be confused with the porn beat.

headline Remember in the eighties when kids were getting words and designs shaved into their heads? That was crazy.

HFR "Hold for release." Not to be confused with "Holy Fuck! Rush!" which is the common newsroom reaction when "Tom Sawyer" comes on the local classic rock station.

inches above the fold Sexual position to be performed only with copy editors. Trust us, it's disgusting.

intern Reason your newspaper doesn't cost twenty-five cents more.

inverted pyramid Common term used to describe the structure of an average news story: the most important or "heaviest" information goes at the beginning, and the least significant or "lightest" at the end. These distinctions are almost impossible to make in stories about Paris Hilton, *American Idol*, or Sarah Palin, so when writing about them, just put shit wherever.

leak Giving story information early or against the desire of its subjects. It's appropriate to place SPOILER WARNING at the beginning of your piece to appease those people who are still upset that we ruined *The Sixth Sense* for them, *Steve.*

lede The opening sentence of a news story; contains the most important information. Named after the ancient Greek queen, which is how the swan came to be the animal totem of journalists.

morgue The room that houses previous issues of a newspaper. Called this because originally it contained piles of dead town criers.

muckraking Publicly exposing misconduct by and/or corruption of public figures or businesses. Dress appropriately; even club soda can't get out muck. And bring your own rake. See: **desk, clean out your.**

news hole Space allocated for news stories in a paper once advertising space is accounted for. See: **Marla in Accounting.**

newsprint Another attempt at running.

objectivity Hey, it's not our place to say if the earth is flat or not.

paper route The once and future job of most newspaper staff.

press release/news release The preferred term for a document announcing a newsworthy event is "news release." "Press release" is a fun game executives play in which they lay off reporters.

press conference/news conference The preferred term for an event where news is announced is a "news conference." A "press conference" is where executives meet to play "press release."

printer's devil Demonic being that once fed on the souls of journalists, replaced during the late twentieth century by global media conglomerates.

propaganda The most sophisticated goose in all of Boston.

"Put the paper to bed" Phrase used to signify that the paper has been sent to press. See: **Marla in Accounting.**

reader Some picky asshole who wants to split hairs.

retraction The act of pushing already-printed newspapers back into the printing press.

revision Yet another well-written story butchered by a certain copy editor named Tim who might find a rattlesnake in his Jetta tonight.

scoop Using a discarded newspaper to pick up your dog's poop during walksies.

source A person who provides you with information for a story. Also, what Darkseid seeks to control in his war with the forces of New Genesis. These are probably not the same thing, though it's best not to get on Darkseid's bad side.

"Stop the presses!" Common phrase uttered by us to your mom when your dad gets home early.

subhead 1. A shorter, one-line headline for a story. 2. The extra head growing out of your editor's left shoulder that everybody tries to pretend isn't a big deal.

Typeface Little-known Batman villain who appeared in several stories in *Detective Comics* in the 1950s.

"unavailable for comment" Euphemism for "stonewalled by the secretary."

widow Line of text separated from the rest of its paragraph and yearning to feel the touch of a man again.

***Wire* report** Did you see that shit with Stringer Bell and Omar? That was intense.

<2>

POLITICS:

WHEN THE

HORSE RACE

LASTS THIRTY MONTHS

I VALUE
MY
GENERAL POINT OF VIEW
MORE THAN
YOURS

At all levels—local, state, federal, the secret one-world regime—politics and government are topics that interest a large number of readers.

There's a simple reason why: Whether it's a tax break for a major corporation, a contract with some company to build moon bombs, or subsidies for car manufacturers, everything government does is funded with taxpayer money. And the crazy thing is, something like 90 percent of your readers—all the ones who don't know or care to know how to get tax breaks, contracts, or subsidies—pay taxes.

One problem, though: the grinding of the government's gears, no matter how big the impact, is boring. There are all kinds of motions and seconds to motions and amendments and amendments to amendments and time yielding and tabling, and it just never ends. Very often you'll attend a four-hour meeting and end up with nothing more than a few brief sentences about someone farting during the Pledge of Allegiance. Nobody even punches anybody or anything! At least, not in the states that aren't Alabama.

Luckily, the government created its own distraction for the national insomnia remedy known as the legislative process: elections! Yes, those ever-satisfying contests where candidates spend months upon months and millions of dollars for the opportunity to sit in an office and field phone calls from senior citizens who don't like having to listen to street sweepers go by at the godawfully late hour of eight p.m.

It's a benefit to both you and your readers that election campaigns now last as long as the actual terms served in office. Writing about elections answers the really important questions: Who's pointing fingers at whom? Who's making accusations about terrorist ties, lack of patriotism, and/or baby killing? Who might have said something that could be construed as racist? And who's denying cheating on his wife despite incontrovertible evidence that he did?

Ah, democracy.

THE BASICS

When writing about political issues, try not to remember that most of your readers will have had their opinions on these topics formed by *Saturday Night Live*, *The Daily Show*, *Glenn Beck*, and other comedy/variety shows. Exceptions to this rule are generally old enough to have voted for Eisenhower. Keep this out of your mind or you'll turn to the drink. Well, more to the drink; you *are* a writer.

Don't try to compete with those television programs on their own comedic turf. First, you're not going to be as funny as they are. Second, your older readers will complain about this young upstart writing stupid things in their paper, and your editors will replace you with that column for bridge players that, like, three people read.

Avoiding political bias in your coverage is vital. Look, we all know that everyone in the news industry is a gay, pagan, atheist commie, but ethically speaking we can't allow our love of drugs, casual sex, and destroying traditional values to get in the way of providing useful political coverage.

So rather than deriding every action by a Republican politician as cryptofascist, racist fearmongering, you should always emphasize the faith and patriotism of a Republican candidate and gloss over the twelve mistresses and the fraud charges.

Likewise, since the public is not ready to be told the truth about Democrats' wild satanic orgies in which the blood of Christian children is used to polish large metal dildos, simply dismiss them as tax-and-spend elitists.

#

Remember that **everything is political**. Movies have political subtexts. Sporting events are national referenda. Television shows contain coded messages telling voters which politicians to support. About the only thing that isn't politically motivated in this country is corporations giving large donations to politicians. They're just helping out their friends with a little mad money.

#

In the interest of pretending to be fair, don't refer to **smaller political parties** with condescending or insulting terms and phrases like "tiny," "cute," "from the land of make-believe," "grade school," "crazy crazies from crazy town," "vaguely amusing," or "the LaRouche movement."

#

When comparing current world leaders, it's very easy to fall into the lazy trap of saying someone is **"worse than Hitler."** This, as we know from documentaries such as *Raiders of the Lost Ark* and *Ilsa, She Wolf of the SS*, is patently false, as

Hitler is worse than everyone in the world, with the possible exception of Eugene Miller of Spokane, Washington.

#

Fairness demands that you consult the pro-tetanus lobby when writing a story on the hazards of rusty nails. Plus, they might be looking to hire an out-of-work journalist in a few months, so why burn bridges?

#

The complex machinations of the mighty are often too byzantine (S.A.T. WORD, ONE HUNDRED POINTS), Machiavellian (DOUBLE-WORD COMBO!), or Brobdingnagian (C-C-C-COMBO BREAKER!!!) for your readers to get through their pretty little heads. Try to use **catchy, sloganlike phrases** that sound good even if they lose nuance. For example, "purchasing distressed assets such as mortgage-backed securities in order to inject capital into failing financial institutions" becomes "bank bailouts," while "diverting monies from arms sales to inimical foreign interests in order to fund guerrilla killers in a politically unstable region" becomes "patriotism."

#

When you need an interesting angle for another boring story about tax cuts, try to find a way to **put a human face on it**. If possible, avoid using flensing knives and staples; kidnapping and mutilation are still crimes in most states, and the delivery boys get huffy if their papers get *too* black and white and red all over. Genetically engineering newsprint to grow humanlike features is a safer bet legally, but remember, that thing is going to be staring back at you while you're flipping through it on the john. And it judges. Oh yes.

#

The difference between "alderman" and "selectman" is that persons holding one office are obligated to fuck donkeys. We'll leave it to you to figure out which one that is.

#

Feel free to editorialize in favor of lower taxes while lamenting how underfunded education and public works programs are. The irony monster isn't going to eat you, we promise.

#

Use "disgraced politician" on first use, "expert political analyst" on later mentions.

SOURCING

When citing undisclosed sources in a political story, use the following terms as a guideline for the level of the source:

- "Source high in the administration": entry-level staffer who glanced at internal memos on the subject of your story. No actual knowledge needed.
- "Source with personal knowledge": administrative assistant who heard office workers or staffers discussing the subject of your story. Lack of personal knowledge required.
- "Source on the inside": drunk guy at a bar ranting about something he heard someone say on "the Hill." No actual conversation required.
- "Unnamed source": janitor willing to confirm something in exchange for a decent-to-OK ham sandwich. Turkey sandwich is an acceptable substitute, but roast beef is not allowed.

ELECTIONS

The most critical part of your political coverage is the campaign, because it is the period in which aspiring politicians make their cases to the public. As the gatekeeper of information, your duty is to provide **clear, nuanced, and unbiased coverage** of each and every politician's core beliefs and ideologies.

At least if the politicians are running as Republicans or Democrats. And have a large enough campaign budget to buy television ad space so that the public is aware of them. Anyone who doesn't meet those criteria can be safely ignored, because, let's face it, they couldn't get elected dog-catcher (which is actually a civil service position filled by the county HR department).

In elections, especially local ones, you'll have to **decide which candidates are viable** and which ones you can mostly ignore because they are insane. Some sure signs of the latter type:

- Their platform consists entirely of changing certain laws because they got arrested one time for trying to steal a flag.

- They wear a law-enforcement badge purchased from a dollar store.

- Their profession is canning and distributing vegetables they grow in their backyard.

- They wear homemade clothes stitched together from washcloths and hand towels.

- They carry around a sword for some reason.

#

You will likely have the opportunity to ask only one or two questions at a **campaign press event**. Limit them to important queries, like what the candidate's favorite beverage is or whether he or she drives a pickup truck.

#

A **political debate** is a great venue for voters to hear all the ways candidates agree with one another and maybe even one or two areas where they have slightly divergent opinions.

Scoring political debates, on the other hand, tends to be a little tougher. In general, you should give a candidate

- one point for every strong policy statement he or she makes;

- one point every time he or she gets a good jab in on an opponent's record;

- one point per wink;

- one point for every minute he or she doesn't look like a deer caught in headlights;

- two points for each time he or she manages to mention his or her opponent's gay daughter, convict son, or collapsing marriage (i.e., the real meat-and-potatoes issues).

ENDORSING POLITICIANS

When it comes time to endorse politicians for public office, you must consider many criteria before putting your organization's weight and reputation behind a candidate. Be sure to note the following points of comparison in your election endorsements:

- candidate's positions on local issues and concerns
- candidate's stance on the wider political arena
- candidate's personal background and professional history
- candidate's Xbox gamer tag and stats (If he's a Wii user, he's clearly not your guy.)
- where candidate stands on the Batman issue: lawless vigilante or freelance policeman?
- how candidate's going to get a chicken into everyone's pot, because, frankly, that seems nigh impossible
- whether candidate's atheism will be a help or a hindrance during his or her term (Ah, just kidding. We all know nobody's gonna elect a non-Christian.)
- the number of neutral and negative feedback ratings on candidate's eBay account
- whether or not candidate is a robot
- how many punches in the stomach candidate can take before vomiting
- the cut of candidate's jib

When conducting **exit-poll interviews**, pick the voters with the most local color. Is there a middle-aged woman wearing a red, white, and blue cat sweatshirt? A man with a tiny dog tucked under his arm? An obnoxious, hemp-wearing, progressive college student? An extremely befuddled elderly man who just wants his coffee and a newspaper already? These are the people whose voices must be heard! Sure, they may not represent the normal people in a community, but normal people are already reading the article. They don't want to hear what they already know.

LEGISLATION

Your job as a political reporter is to inform your readers how the decisions made by politicians will affect their lives. (That may seem self-evident, but this chapter of the book is likely to be read by television personalities, so we need to SPEAK. VERY. SLOWLY.)

Use **colorful metaphors** to present political subjects in terms more familiar to your readers. *Saints alive! Mitch McConnell has got Harry Reid in a figure-four leg lock of fiscal responsibility! It looks like the D-Team is taking the fall this match! Wait! Here's John Kerry climbing the ropes . . . and he's carrying the folding chair of a strong military service record! Holy smokes!*

#

When reporting on the creation and passage of a **county/state/federal budget**, most writers will simply skim the bill to find out who took the biggest cuts, who got the biggest increases, and which employees got raises. But only you know that extracting the first three digits of every line item will reveal the secret ur-Constitution containing the alien technology that the shadow Congress will use to fly America to Uranus in 2015.

#

Political reporters must have a firm understanding of **how a bill becomes a law**. First, a draft of the legislation is drawn up and presented to the House of Representatives. The merits of the bill are debated in committee, and attachments and amendments are added to the bill. Then, in an unholy mockery of science, the bill is brought to life through the blood sacrifice of twelve congressional pages and placed on the steps of the Capitol, where it must entertain passersby with songs. If the songs meet with the public's approval, the bill is passed into law. And twelve new pages are sought.

#

It is a widely held misconception that the legislative branch writes the laws, the executive branch enforces them, the judicial branch interprets them, and the public at large votes people into those offices to represent its will. The system is in fact far more complex, as the following list demonstrates:

- declaring war: at the discretion of the executive branch.
- deciding who gets to marry whom: popular vote.
- increasing taxes: forbidden.
- spending income: at the discretion of the executive branch.
- deciding who gets to be president: the Supreme Court.

NOTES ON A SCANDAL

When questioning a politician about a scandal in which he or she is involved, you may interpret that politician's responses as follows:

"I didn't do it." = "I totally did it."

"My wife is standing by me in this time of crisis." = "I'm gay."

"History will vindicate me." = "Oh God, I will forever be remembered as 'the mayor who schtupped a cocker spaniel.' "

"I did not take that bribe." = "I grabbed that money like it was a drunk secretary at the office party."

"I have absolutely no connection to that woman." = "Phone records will show that I sexted this woman approximately seventy-four times a day."

"I will not resign." = "Please forward my mail to this township in Mexico, beginning immediately."

"I did not misappropriate any funds donated to my campaign . . ." = ". . . which will continue as I drive from county to county in this swell new Bentley Continental GTZ."

"Yes, I did it. I take full responsibility." = "I'm really not cut out for politics."

"No comment." = "Not only did I do it, but wait till you hear about the rest of the sick shit that hasn't been turned up by the press yet."

SUBHEADLINEGATE

Every journalist dreams of breaking the big story like Bob Woodward and Carl Bernstein did with the Watergate break-in. How did Woodward and Bernstein, now the two most famous newspapermen in history (the third most famous, just so you know, is Jayson Blair) do it? By relying on the nuts and bolts of journalism: digging up sources, double sourcing every fact, taking personal risks, knocking on doors, wearing out shoe leather, and burning the midnight oil.

But that's the kind of exhausting hard work that would require you to get your ass out of your comfy office chair. (It's also worth noting that Woodward and Bernstein could have cut all that work down to almost nothing if they had had the Internet. After all, we just Googled "Who broke in to the Watergate hotel?" and got an answer in less than a second: G. Gordon Liddy and Monica Lewinsky.) So, what do you do if you want to become a famous journalist without doing all that work?

When you boil down Woodward and Bernstein's achievement to its most basic elements, the key was clearly coming up with a marketable, memorable name for the scandal they broke. Now you can easily ride on the coattails of great journalists simply by adding the suffix "-gate" to your scandal. Hell, it doesn't even have to be a real scandal—just look at how well it worked for such made-up shit as "Travelgate," "Climategate," and "Semen-on-the-dress-gate."

Therefore, to get ready for the next big (or small) scandal that comes your way, you should keep a list of potential

"-gate" titles. Here is a list of past and future ones to help you get started:

Colgategate: That senator's very inappropriate use of a tube of toothpaste.

Collategate: How that one damn administrative assistant can never get your copies in the right order.

Fencegate: Yeah, we really need to get around to installing that. We have a three-day weekend coming up, so we'll do it then.

Gatemouthgate: Blues guitarist accused of doing woman wrong.

Gatesgate: The conspiracy among Bill Gates, Henry Louis Gates, and Daryl Gates to take over the world with a weather-control satellite.

Gatogate: The Mexican cat-boxing scandal that nearly brought down Vicente Fox's administration.

Masturgate: Keep this one in your back pocket; you know you're going to be using it someday.

Skategate: You know it was those punk kids who wrecked the statue of the town founder in the park. If only you could prove it.

Stargategate: That whole *Atlantis* thing.

GLOSSARY

activist judges Those judges whose rulings contradict your political beliefs. For judges whose rulings you agree with, use "strict constitutionalists."

anarchist That annoying little shit down the street with the torn white T-shirts who plays his music too loud.

bicameral legislature When C-SPAN sends two video teams to Congress instead of just the one.

Bill of Rights A document describing the fundamental rights of rich, white, male landowners. Sometimes the rights are extended to other alleged "citizens," but c'mon, who're we kidding?

bipartisanship Any demonstration of cooperation between the two major politic— Ha, no, we can't say that with a straight face.

Bull Moose Party Short-lived party that supported Teddy Roosevelt's 1912 presidential campaign. So named because Roosevelt won the party's nomination by killing a bull moose with his bare hands. The party soon died out when no other aspiring candidate could fulfill the nomination requirement.

Chief of Staff Nickname your mom gave us last night.

cloakroom The area from which lobbyists and congressional aides use captured Romulan stealth technology to direct action on the Senate floor.

cloture Harry Reid's safe word.

Communist Party Preferred political leaning of most members of the American media.

Congressional Record Record of outstanding

achievements accomplished during congressional sessions. *The Congressional Record for keg stands is currently held by John "The Kegmeister" Boehner, at four minutes and fifteen seconds.*

Defense, Department of Formerly known as the Department of War. The name change in 1949 was intended to convey a less aggressive posture to people in the various nations America was bombing the bejesus out of at the time.

deficit The worst thing in the world if it occurs during a Democratic president's term; no big thang during a Republican's.

DINO Nickname for singer and actor Dean Martin. As the comic foil in a number of films costarring Jerry Lewis, Martin was frequently cast as a man who claimed to support the concept of a single-payer health-care system but consistently voted against the increases in corporate taxes necessary to pay for one.

election A contest for political office in which all candidates damage one another's credibility in an effort to make voters more confident.

electoral votes We don't really understand how these work either.

factoids Lies.

Federal Communications Commission Government agency responsible for keeping us safe from cartoons and swearing rappers.

FEMA A locally produced, ecofriendly feminine-hygiene product popular in the greater suburbs of Washington DC.

filibuster The political equivalent of taking the ball and going home if you don't get your way. Even though the ball actually belongs to another kid and he has more friends than you, you still get your way because your friends keep calling the popular kid a socialist.

First Amendment That portion of the U.S. Constitution that allows us to write terrible things in this glossary about prominent political figures without fear of retribution. Thanks, Founding Fathers! John Quincy Adams sucks!

fiscal year Like a dog year, but for money.

flat tax The solution to all of our problems.

Founding Fathers Always capitalize out of respect for the wise men of two hundred years ago whose opinions on Internet porn and the right to own a bazooka guide us today.

gerrymandering Changing the boundaries of electoral districts to secure election results for a particular candidate or political party. Not to be confused with "jerrymathering," the act of changing the boundaries of the area in which the Beaver is allowed to ride his bicycle.

habeas corpus Latin for "let the court have the body," most famously employed by Chief Justice Roger B. Taney during *State of New York v. Honey Hugemelons* (1858).

hard money Contributions from the porn lobby to campaigns or parties.

impeachment Procedure in which a politician convicted of wrongdoing is taken to the town square and tied to a post and citizens throw peaches at him until he dies.

inaugural balls Condition suffered by a president-elect who has waited too long between election and assuming the presidency.

laissez-faire Alan Greenspan's safe word.

lame duck A politician who has broken a leg in a fall or other accident and can no longer serve out his term. Such politicians are taken out behind the barn and shot, and their bodies sent to the glue factory for processing.

liberal media Channel 22 in Oakland, California, broadcast intermittently between 1:00 and 5:00 a.m., according to eyewitness accounts.

Lincoln, Abraham Sixteenth president of the United States. Issued the Emancipation Proclamation abolishing slavery. Ended the secession of the Confederate States of America during the Civil War. Assassinated in 1865. Dude was hardcore.

lobbyist A person who stands around in a lobby waiting for politicians to come out. Once they do, the lobbyist hides money under a table somewhere and challenges the politicians to find it. This usually involves a series of arrows written on masking tape and left in areas of increasing difficulty to find. Eventually, the politicians are whittled down to a handful, often resorting to violence to ensure victory. In the end, the last man standing collects his money and holds it aloft beneath the rostrum, chest heaving, covered in sweat and bruises. And thus, check-cashing stores remain in business.

Majority Whip Preferred sandwich spread in the greater DC area.

minority-majority district A political district where racial or ethnic minorities make up a majority of the voting public. Rare and difficult to find, much like the majestic unicorn.

moonbats Giant bats . . . from the MOON. Their sonar doesn't seem to work properly on earth, causing them to flail about wildly and bump into things.

motion A parliamentary move a member of a governing body may wish to put in your ocean.

Mr. Smith The third-floor janitor in the Capitol who always gets a good-natured ribbing and is not at all tired of it, as far as we know.

mutually assured destruction A mysterious sexual technique pioneered and refined by brave NSA agents in 1952.

national conventions Gatherings at which members of a political party announce candidacies, set party policies, and raise local prostitution revenues by approximately 225 percent.

neocon Short for "neoconservative," an adherent of contemporary right-wing philosophies who favors black clothes, sunglasses, and long coats.

October surprise Mom's delicious pumpkin soufflé, widely acknowledged to have cost Jimmy Carter the 1980 election.

Ombudsman Superhero mascot of American Jah Buddha, a faith-based, pro-marijuana political action group.

PAC Groups of people engaged in investigating Tupac Shakur's untimely demise.

Perot, Ross A prank presidential candidate in the 1992 election who garnered nationwide attention and fostered the mistaken belief that a third party could challenge the traditional two-party system. Perot ran again in 1996, demonstrating that one should really learn not to drive a joke into the ground.

pork-barrel spending Any legislation workshopped over the Tuesday lunch special at Reggie's Bottomless BBQ off K Street.

press pool Brian Williams's bitchin' Olympic-size backyard swimming facility. Barbecue this weekend, WOOOOOO!

pundit Mugger with a penchant for wordplay. Sadly, punditry is not yet a death-penalty offense.

quid pro quo Latinism meaning "How about a little sugar for Senator Huggybear, chickie?"

quorum John Boehner's safe word.

Rasmussen Polling service used to determine public opinion on political topics. Also, rejected villain from *Die Hard 2*.

Reagan, Ronald Fortieth president of the United States. Made movies with chimpanzees. We're not making fun. We actually think that's kind of awesome.

rear loading An intensified effort to raise the public's awareness of a candidate shortly before an election. See: **Larry Craig.**

recount The end of an election for sore losers.

Republicrat See: **Demoblican; Demopublican; Redemopubcrat; Derepopublicracan.**

RINO Former U.S. representative Rex Crushman (R-Mich.), a pro-choice, pro–gun control fiscal conservative who was also a fucking rhinoceros.

SCOTUS! The Beast with Nine Faces, Dread Lord of the Sixty-Ninth Dimension, and Master of Darkness, praise his awful name and all blood sacrifice be unto him. His symbol shall be the ebon robe and his names shall be legion. And Alito.

scrum An informal press conference assembled outside a legislative session. Named for the toxic slime trails left behind afterward.

Smithsonian Institution Museum founded by James

Smithson to popularize America's scientific and cultural accomplishments. For simplicity's sake, refer to it as "the place where they keep Fonzie's leather jacket."

snake oil The substance that lubricates the gears of the democratic process.

Speaker of the House As of this writing, a quad stack of 150-watt Kenwoods on wall brackets with a bitchin' subwoofer mounted under the podium.

Sub Committee The congressional committee on "How Delicious Are Submarine Sandwiches, Huh?" Sometimes informally called "Hoagie Caucus."

suffrage What men have to put up with since they started allowing women to vote.

sunshine laws Vary from state to state and even by municipality. Seattle's are among the strictest in the United States.

swing voter A voter that goes both ways, if you know what we mean.

talking points See: **factoids.**

Vice President Dude officially in charge of going down to the skate shop every month and picking up enough copies of the new issue for everyone.

voter Senior citizen and/or campaign contributor.

Whig Party Eighteenth-century antipopulist group that believed the legislative branch should wield more power than the executive. Now chiefly remembered for inspiring Greg Dulli.

wingnuts Genetically modified legumes capable of independent flight, though they tend to stay together in impenetrable groups close to the ground.

<3>

ENTERTAINMENT:

THE GLITZ,

THE GLAMOUR,

THE DEATH OF THE SUPEREGO

WE ARE YOUR
BETTERS
8 PM/ 7 CENTRAL
ONLY ON
THE TV NETWORK

The onset of the Internet, coupled with an explosion of entertainment news programs and magazines, has people spending more time than ever reading and learning about their favorite celebrities—likely even more time than they spend actually watching movies or listening to music.

This voracious appetite for news, reviews, previews, interviews, rumors, speculation, and conjecture has to be fed by someone. That's where you, the freelance entertainment writer, come in. After all, *People* magazine doesn't write itself (though there are rumors it gained sentience during Brad Pitt and Angelina Jolie's affair).

But how do you get the attention you deserve as an entertainment writer? How do you interview a celebrity you couldn't care less about? How do you talk shit about a movie and still get into free previews? How do you write a review of a new album and make it as much about yourself as about the music? How do you keep saying the same things every award season without anyone noticing? How do you look at yourself in the mirror every morning?

When facing this last question, we think it's best to recall this old joke: A man's walking home from work one day when he sees another man shoveling elephant dung at a traveling circus. The man stops and says to the elephant keeper, "My goodness! That seems like a horrible job! Have you considered finding a better way to make money?" To which the elephant keeper replies, "What, and give up show business?"

MOVIES

Movie Criticism

Be certain to use some sort of **cute iconography** to denote how many points a film receives. Stars are popular to the point of cliché, along with film reels and "thumbs up." A unique scheme—"underpaid projectionists," perhaps, or "crying babies"—helps attract attention to your reviews. Genre-specific objects can be used as well, such as severed heads for horror films, adorable puppies for children's films, or brave women dying of fatal diseases for Oscar-baiting dramas released in December.

#

Be sure to give every **Tyler Perry movie** a five-star review because you feel guilty and embarrassed about not having heard of him until a couple of years ago.

#

Be aware that you are, by and large, useless. You're not going to convince anyone to go see the really worthwhile movies, because they're all about Forbidden Sherpa Love and nobody will pay for that. You're also not going to convince anyone not to see *Boob Train IV* because if those people had any critical sense they wouldn't think of going in the first place.

Your main job, then, is to steer people toward things that are "better than you expected" and away from things that are "not as good as you hoped."

#

Use a possessive proper noun in the title of a **movie remake** to convey crushing disappointment (e.g., *Tim Burton's Planet of the Apes*).

Your Guide to Quote Whoring!

Looking for a leg up in the vicious world of movie reviewing? Quote whoring—the honorable profession of providing gushing blurbs for movie ads—is a great way to catch the eye of the PR flacks.

BLOGGER, PLEASE!

Not sure how to get started? No worries! Grab a stack of studio PR contacts, buy yourself a website, and get ready to turn your laptop into a one-stop quote emporium for every movie you can just barely afford to see. Movie studios couldn't care less if they're quoting Elvis Mitchell or MyDogElvisReviewsMovies.net, and without an editor breathing down your neck about ethical standards and responsibility to your readership, you can really let yourself go wild.

Maybe *Jennifer's Body* really is the best movie you've seen since *The Thin Red Line*. Maybe Shia LaBeouf's performance in *Transformers: Revenge of the Fallen* really did remind you of the last summer day you spent with your great-grandpa before he died of lung cancer. Stranger things have happened!

MAKE WAY FOR ELLIPSES . . . [AND BRACKETS, TOO!]

Be sure to place all negative sentiment at the beginning of a sentence, where it can be easily discarded. For example, "I didn't really think Edward Norton was giving

MOVIE RATINGS

The ratings used by the Motion Picture Association of America are:

G General audiences. All ages; may contain cartoon animals, toys, fish, or cars that speak. Specifically designed to traumatize children.

PG Parental guidance suggested but not really expected. There may be some swears and decapitation. For kids' movies, this is "the hard stuff."

PG-13 Parents strongly cautioned. Definitely swears, strong violence, maybe the suggestion of boobs. Major studios refer to this rating as "cash money." Independent studios refer to this rating as "impossible."

R Restricted; children under seventeen permitted only with an adult or if they say they have an adult with them or, hell, they've got money, let 'em in. Quite likely a chance to sit next to your mom and look at boobs on a twenty-foot screen.

NC-17 No one under seventeen admitted, wall-to-wall drunk-dad-level-three swearing. Eyes cut with razor blades. People "doing it." Some women may have three (or more) boobs.

his best performance ever in *The Incredible Hulk*" can, with a simple wave of a studio PR department's magic punctuation wand, turn into "Edward Norton['s] . . . best performance ever!"

MY GOD, IT'S REALLY FULL OF STARS!

Honestly, it's easy to think of reasons to give five stars to a movie. Wasn't Steve Martin's makeup in *The Pink Panther II* fantastic? Think of all the hard work the catering crew did lugging bagels and lox down Forty-sixth Street on a muggy fall afternoon in New York City. Remember, it would be cruel not to recognize all the craftsmen (and a few women!) who put their backs into four or five hours of work every day.

CELEBRITIES

When discussing the **private lives of celebrities**, be sure to mention if they are married or dating. If they are married to or dating another celebrity, mention this as often as possible. It is not necessary to contract their names into a single identifier, but if you must, the celebrity with the most to lose goes first, e.g., Brangelina, Bennifer, Kermiggy.

Great care should be taken when discussing the private lives of **gay and lesbian celebrities**.

When referencing the romantic life of a closeted celebrity, be sure to only use gender-neutral pronouns. "I am dating a wonderful man; he's a lawyer" becomes "I am dating a wonderful person. They're a lawyer."

When the celebrity in question is not openly gay but everyone knows he or she is gay anyway, feel free to refer to his or her partner with an innocuous title; by this point everyone knows what "personal trainer" and "secretary" really mean. Be careful not to overidentify the partner; noting that the "personal trainer" is also a bartender at Coop's Greased Piston Bar and Baths is considered "giving the game away."Never refer to the partners of openly gay celebrities, because ew, that's gross.

#

Celebrities accused of crimes are either obviously guilty or obviously innocent, regardless of evidence, and your articles about their yearlong trials should reflect this truth.

#

Keep in mind that celebrities exist in a world that may seem similar to ours but in which the relative importance of crimes has been completely reversed. If a celebrity has a few drinks and trips over a curb, you should interview the most famous therapist you can for insight on the celebrity's crippling addiction and send a photographer out to capture the candlelight vigil.

If, on the other hand, a celebrity with a ski slope's worth of coke in his nose crashes an Army-surplus Humvee into a school for hemophiliac orphans while driving the corpse of his personal assistant to the La Brea Tar Pits, you should be sure to light him from a flattering angle when he makes his comeback speech after a forty-three-minute stint in a minimum-security prison and day spa.

#

Pick from the following list of words when describing an actress who has had too much Botox:

- shellacked
- frozen
- immobile
- smooth
- unwrinkled
- Nicole Kidman

#

When writing about **celebrity fashion**, be sure to highlight the most expensive and ridiculous items in order to give the masses something to strive for: *Audrina Patridge was spotted at the Ivy carrying a Mulberry bag made of silverback gorilla hide.*

#

When writing about **celebrity pregnancies**, be sure to detail how quickly the celebrities lose the weight after giving birth: *Heidi Klum had yet another baby two weeks ago, and already she is wearing a bejeweled bikini in the Victoria's Secret fashion show. She is currently expecting another baby in two weeks.*

#

If you go through **video footage frame by frame**, you should be able to find an image of a celebrity squinting with one eye shut, sticking his or her tongue out oddly, or otherwise pulling some kind of strange face. Print it, run it!

#

When composing your story about a **celebrity being a raging dick** to a store employee or restaurant staffer, be sure to ignore any possible evidence that the employee in question may have been asking for it.

#

If a celebrity throws a telephone at a guy, that's news. If a celebrity is looking thin and/or fat, that's news. If a celebrity has sex on tape, that's news. If a celebrity gets mad on a movie set, that's news. If a celebrity dies in an untimely fashion, stop getting all up in their business, you vultures!

#

Caption all photos of **cellulite, stretch marks, or varicose veins** with the simple word "HU-MAN!" and a doodle of someone pointing and screaming.

#

Remember, when writing about a celebrity for an **online audience**, save your readers time by linking directly to nude photos of him or her.

#

"Exhaustion" and "dehydration" are both spelled with a silent innuendo.

#

Movie stars with eight kids are great parents who love kids. People in the newspaper or on reality television with eight kids are freak shows. Regular people with eight kids are parasites who should be sterilized by the government.

Celebrity Interviews—How to Totally Kick Ass at Them

Never dress nicer than your celebrity interview subject; you want to make him or her comfortable and reinforce his or her innate sense of superiority. Since your celebrity will be spending most of the interview staring at your feet and mumbling, you should wear unfashionable, slightly beat-up shoes. The pair you have on right now are fine.

If you are a male writer conducting an interview with an actress, be sure to spend at least three (but no more than seven) introductory paragraphs describing just how badly you want to bang her. If you are a female writer interviewing George Clooney, bring protection.

Greet your celebrity with a bone-crushing handshake and a loud "HOWDY DO!" or something similar while maintaining constant, uncomfortable eye contact. This will catch your celebrity's attention.

Asking nouveau riche pop or sports stars when we can see their multiple sports cars, wide-screen televisions, mansions, etc., on the auction block is considered bad form and should be avoided.

Inquire in detail about a **celebrity's phobia**. Bonus: bring live animals or pictures of the phobia subject to the interview.

Don't be afraid to ask **rhetorical questions** that have nothing to do with the film or project the celebrity is promoting, e.g., *Mariah Carey, if you could choose three figures from history to help you battle an army of ghost Nazis, who would you choose?*

Never say an actor or actress farted loudly throughout an interview. Instead say he or she "paused thoughtfully."

Keep in mind that your celebrity interview subject is contractually obligated to promote a film or project in a marathon of interviews—known as a **"junket"**—and premieres that leaves him utterly exhausted. Your interview may be his twentieth of the day. He's tired and impatient, making this the perfect time to screw with him:

- Repeat the last question, but LOUDER.
- Ask, "So you don't remember me, do you? You really have no idea who I am?"
- Stare intently at a fixed point just behind the celebrity's head.
- Strike him! Strike him suddenly, without warning!
- Ask him about his time singing backup for Bette Midler. Repeatedly.
- Pose an insulting question in Vietnamese or Icelandic.

Celebrity Obituaries

When writing the initial summary of the deceased's accomplishments, try to **accent the positive** (". . . whose single 'Pretty Hula Girl' made it to #97 on the Billboard Top 100 in 1957") over the infamous (". . . was found walking naked down Hollywood Boulevard in 1974 carrying the severed head of a prostitute"), as the latter points are better discussed in detail within the body of the article.

Show an **appropriate level of respect** by substituting "controversial personality" for "complete asshole" and "eccentric" for "utterly batshit."

Other phrases to commit to memory include "in the

midst of planning a comeback," "spoke to a generation," and "autoerotic asphyxiation."

As readers' cultural memory will rarely extend past the previous six months, contextualize the deceased's contributions to his or her field with **comparisons to currently popular entertainers**: *Her pioneering work as a cool jazz vocalist made her the Hannah Montana of her time.*

TELEVISION

If a network describes a new program as "like nothing you've ever seen before," **review last year's hit shows** for a refresher on what this show is probably going to be like.

#

When a beloved sitcom ends, be sure to discuss the inevitably successful **movie projects and television spin-offs** that the stars will move on to—even though this has never been the case.

#

When covering any kind of convention dedicated to a **science-fiction or fantasy television show**, home in on freakiest attendees and imply heavily that they are indicative of the entire fan base. The furrier, more skintight-costumed, and/or more heavyset the people, the better. This rule also applies to comic book conventions.

#

For the 2011 edition of this guide, *According to Jim* is no longer available as the default television show about which to marvel at the fact that it's still on TV. Please update to *Two and a Half Men*.

The Super Bowl

The Super Bowl is an important entertainment event deserving of special attention, but not because of the game.

Rather, the most important part of the program is the ads. On the other 364 days of the year people hate television ads, calling them obnoxious and intrusive. But on Super Bowl Sunday digital video recorders become Bizarro TiVos, employed to record the event so that not a single precious ad is lost. Viewers tune in specifically to see what delights Pepsi, Budweiser, and Paramount Pictures come up with. Like everyone else, you will be expected to discuss this festival of short features as though you just got back from Cannes.

Here are some tips for writing about the Super Bowl. These rules will never need revising:

- Make sure to open your article with an observation about how surprising it was that viewers were focused on the ads rather than the game. It might seem unnecessary since that's how every single article on the Super Bowl for the past thirty years has started, but Old Gus down in printing tells us it's good luck.

- Avoid marveling at the fact that screenwriters, actors, directors, and other dedicated artists are using their craft to get people to eat a hamburger made entirely of bacon. After all, you're the one who thought J-school was a good idea.

- Super Bowl commercials often feature past-their-prime celebrities making an unexpected but welcome second shot at relevance, but you should resist referring to the ads as "Tarantino-esque" unless they feature lingering shots of an actress's feet and at least one uncomfortable use of the "N" word.

MUSIC

When writing about a popular new band, use **superlative terms** such as "band of the decade" and "album of the year" in your fawning profile. A few months later, be sure to write about the same band's "droning" and how they're "no Vampire Weekend" with no irony whatsoever.

#

Due to the recent death of Michael Jackson, we will not make jokes concerning him. He was a wonderful performer whose music touched many hearts, and he will be dearly missed.

#

In reviews of **hip-hop albums**, be sure to use words such as "tight," "flow," and "thumpin'" so that readers will know that you, a college-educated suburbanite who wears Buddy Holly glasses, are down with the streets.

#

Nobody is the next Beatles. On the off chance someone or some band is the next Beatles, it's unlikely anyone is going to realize it ahead of time. Instead, all **rock 'n' roll quartets** should be referred to as "the Beatles on steroids."

#

If writing for a po-faced, twee, **alternative music magazine or website**, be sure to throw in the occasional T-Pain or Adam Lambert record review. They're the faded county fair T-shirt from 1985 of your chosen critical genre.

#

Due to the recent death of Prince we will not make jokes concerning him. He was a wonderful performer whose music touched many hearts, and he will be dearly missed.

#

When writing pieces on how bands like Radiohead, Pearl Jam, and Nine Inch Nails have successfully released their records online, sometimes for free, never point out that the only reason for the success of their venture was a massive preexisting fan base. This way the hundreds of lesser bands following their lead will quickly be squashed by waves of piracy they can never hope to combat with their middling levels of popularity. There are way too many bands out there, anyway, and you can only listen to so many albums in a week.

#

Oh hey, Prince is still alive? In that case: Man, what a fucking weirdo that dude is!

AWARD SEASON

Award shows are fertile ground for coverage. Be sure to hit all these angles:

- Why everyone will be watching this year.
- Why no one will be watching this year.
- How interminably long the show is, not including the two hours of added pre- and postshow coverage.

- What the celebrities were wearing and why it was so ugly.
- Who showed up with whom, who didn't show up with his or her spouse/longtime lover, and who lowered herself to be seen with Rob Schneider.
- Who got snubbed and whom he or she plans to beat up about it.
- All of Jack Nicholson's reactions.
- Who was drunk, who was high, and who almost died.
- Reasons the musical numbers just don't work with Middle America, such as "too gay" or "not gay enough."
- How the host was the worst since David Letterman.
- How the host was the best since David Letterman.
- The great, terrible, or great-terrible rapport of the presenters.
- How great all the after parties are and how none of the people watching will ever get to go to anything so amazing in their whole lives.
- The one nominee who made a sour face when he or she didn't win.
- Maybe who won, if you still have time to get around to it.

Once an actor wins an Oscar, it is appropriate to refer to that actor as **"Academy Award winner."** It is also entirely appropriate to grit your teeth and roll your eyes when referring to "Academy Award winner Cuba Gooding Jr." See also: Mira Sorvino, Diablo Cody, the mom from *The Partridge Family*, *Schindler's List*.

#

It is a mathematical certainty that all Americans will eventually win either a Grammy or an Emmy; therefore, treat these awards with an appropriate level of significance.

#

Be sure to **exaggerate the value of the Golden Globes** in predicting the Academy Award winners. Do not mention that the only reason anyone even goes to the Golden Globes is for the free booze. You do not want to piss off the Hollywood Foreign Press Association because they will shank you just for looking at them sideways.

THE FINE ARTS

Remember how you once strung together a bunch of meaningless ten-dollar words for that college report on *Ethan Frome*? Now imagine getting paid for writing the same report, only this time about interpretive dance. Such is the life of the "fine arts" critic, whose journalistic function is to binge on free wine and cheese while assuaging his editor's guilt over publishing a five-star review of the latest Kevin James comedy.

The fine-arts critic operates within a comfortable little bubble, safe in the knowledge that no one will ever read his or her thoughts on whatever modern art installation or avant-garde performance piece has recently rolled into town. This grants the writer considerable latitude in discussing such things as a postmodern dance recital based on the Thirty Years' War (with jazz hands representing the Defenestration of Prague), though there are guidelines to be followed.

Avoid using phrases such as "it cried out to me" and "it sang to my soul," as they border on obvious parody and risk upsetting the *merlot et Brie* cart. Instead **use vague adjectives** like "uplifting," "transcendent," or "rockalicious" to convey those sentiments.

It is no longer necessary to review any more stage performances of *The Rocky Horror Show* or to even remind readers that the show still exists. The ones who need to know already do. The people who don't know would be happier not knowing. That's valuable ad space you're filling up.

In reviewing a **show at an art gallery**, focus on pieces that use excrement or bodily fluids as part of the materials. If no such pieces are present, find a likely piece and, while no one's looking, "apply yourself," if you get our meaning.

When writing on **classical Greek statues**, a certain amount of decorum is expected; thus, please attempt to minimize commentary on any given statue's "bodacious tatas" or "tiny wiener."

If reviewing a **stage production not subsidized by Disney**, hold off for an hour or so. It will probably be shut down by the time you hit "send."

Alternatively, just write that it's a deeply resonant examination of the fractured American family. (Someone may write in to correct you that Henrik Ibsen was Norwegian, but you can either respond that his themes are timeless and not fettered by geography or just throw the letter away.) If there's a TV or movie star in the play, his or her performance was surprisingly nuanced. Look at that, you wrote a review! Go celebrate with a drink.

VIDEOGAMES

Because videogame journalism has only begun to emerge from the nerd ghetto, it is important to strike the correct tone when writing such pieces. Be sure to let the readers know that you are not some basement-dwelling troglodyte by making **at least a dozen references per review** to your prodigious partying skills, expensive home theater system, or incredible sexual prowess: *After fragging the hapless noob into gibs, I turned to my hot blonde wife, Candi, and asked what she thought about the game's frame rate and HD resolution.*

(These asides can, and probably will, be entirely fictional but are important to offset the boasts about your fifty-fourth-level night elf ranger.)

Though some may characterize it as morbid, **try to predict the number of murders** likely to result from teens

ALWAYS REMEMBER

The quality of a movie is directly correlated to its gross box-office take. How good an album is depends on the number of times it is stolen. A stage play's worth is determined by what movies the lead actors have been in, as well as whether Mel Brooks is involved.

playing the game. Then, months later, when you report on the inevitable murders, you can let readers know how close you were.

GLOSSARY

ABC Acceptable in all references to American Broadcasting Company. Also acceptable: The House That Arthur Fonzarelli Built.

actor Use to refer to a male performer in movies, TV shows, plays, etc. who has talent. For others, use "dude." *Actor Ben Kingsley is attached to star alongside dude Keanu Reeves.*

actress Use only to refer to Meryl Streep, as she has trademarked the word. For young female performers, use "starlet." For older female performers, use "I think she's had some work done."

ad-lib Abbreviation for "adding liberally"; describes an actor who starts making shit up on the spot, either because he has forgotten his lines or because he has just plain had it with this stupid play.

album side (archaic) In general, approximately one half of a Pink Floyd song or one quarter of a Grateful Dead song.

alley Where you find broken and desperate actors and actresses. See: **Alley, Kirstie.**

alternative (music) Mainstream with a goatee and a useless liberal-arts degree.

associate producer His check cleared, so he's in the credits.

avant-garde Will involve nudity.

backward masking An urban legend that secret satanic messages were placed on rock albums and would only be revealed by playing the record backward on a turntable. Propagated by record labels and record player needle manufacturers to encourage replacement sales for ruined records and needles, respectively. Mostly forgotten today, as most albums are on compact disc and are far more terrifying played forward than any supposed backward satanic message could be.

ballet Buncha skinny broads runnin' back an' forth across the stage on their tippy toes pretending to be ducks or some shit, and guys in pants that are *way* too tight sometimes pick 'em up and throw 'em around, and there's some music playin' and who knows what the hell all this is about, but the wife had to go and see it and God knows you gotta keep her happy, but just look at that. Capitalized when referring to organizations such as Spandau Ballet.

Best Boy Quite simply the greatest and most amazing boy in the world! Strange visitor from a distant galaxy, Best Boy has come to our planet to ensure cinematic excellence!

Broadway Street in New York where large-scale musicals are performed, always featuring expensive special effects because if people actually cared about the singing, opera would still be a viable art form.

classical (music) The Dead White Men Hit Parade.

Clear Channel See: **Skynet.**

December Any movie released outside of this month

should not be taken seriously from a critical standpoint.

Diamond, Neil Avoid describing as "mesmerizingly sexy" and "the greatest entertainer on the planet," as these are redundant.

director The one person responsible for making the entire film.

drum solo The middle three hours of "In-A-Gadda-Da-Vida."

Fitty Rapper 50 Cent; when lowercased, someone who is prone to fits.

foxy Attractive, especially female celebrity. Do not use to describe Monica Bellucci, as "Monica Bellucci" is Italian for "foxy."

frak Should only be used if you're fighting Cylons. Are you fighting Cylons? Yeah, didn't think so.

free verse Poetry written by lazy people.

fun for the whole family Loaded with fart jokes.

gold/platinum/diamond record Often mistaken for awards given to musicians for album sales, these are CDs and records that simply won't play.

has-been Stars whose fame has long since passed them by, and yet here you are still writing about them and calling them "has-beens," smart guy.

Hollyweird Lazy shorthand; use liberally.

Hollywood Acceptable as a general term for the U.S. movie industry, though the more accurate descriptor is "Vancouver."

in medias res Latin term meaning "We forgot to write the beginning, so we'll just start in the middle, if that's OK with you."

JCVD Shorthand for action movie star Jean-Claude Van Damme.

JCvD Shorthand for landmark legal case *Johnny Cash v. Dracula* (1974).

Jon and Kate For first mention; "Jesus, ENOUGH" afterward.

jumping the shark Point at which a TV show crosses over into self-parody and begins its decline. Billionaire industrialist Xerxes Hollandaise III has a standing offer of a ten-thousand-dollar reward to the first person to declare that a show has jumped the shark, which is why people fall all over themselves to do it. The term comes from an actual shark-jumping stunt in season five of the show *Happy Days*. *Happy Days* lasted eleven seasons.

laugh track The tormented screeches of the damned, trapped in sitcom soundtracks for all eternity.

lost its luster Used to describe a movie sequel, follow-up album, revival performance, or television season that is less enjoyable than previous installments, especially if made of iron or chrome.

Mr. T People who type out "Mister" are fools to be pitied.

off-Broadway Not good enough to play in a large theater; may involve nudity.

oldies Vintage hits by Hall & Oates, Billy Joel, and, as of last week, Nirvana.

paparazzi Plural form of "paparazzo," which is Italian for "man with camera who is hit at low speed by car driven by a drunk starlet."

Polanski, Roman Helpful litmus test to gauge the relative worthlessness of film artisans you previously had respect for.

producer Supplies drugs and alcohol in quantities sufficient to tame the talent.

product placement The gratuitous use of Coca-Cola® or the Apple iPhone® or Rice Krispies® or the Xbox 360® or the sleek stylings of the Jaguar XK® or the Sony Bravia® HD TV in a film or television show in exchange for payment, for no reason other than advertising a particular product, like the delicious Hershey's® chocolate bar or the rich, flavorful taste of Marlboro® cigarettes.

public access A carnival freak show without the smell.

radio Capitalize when referring to an official government station such as Radio Moscow or Radio Clash.

reality television Fully scripted dramedies starring people you couldn't be paid to hang out with in real life.

red carpet See: **Shirley MacLaine, Nicole Kidman, Ron Howard.**

R.E.M. All caps, with three periods, just like the band: the period when they were good, the period when they were popular, and the current one, when they're neither.

remastered Term used to get consumers to buy the same album more than once.

reunion Use to describe the reassembling of a band under its old name, even though it only includes one original member.

revival A fifty-year-old play that was corny when it was released but that has become cheap to license.

road company When the understudies of a musical's cast are allowed to perform in Chicago and Los Angeles for people who can't figure out how to buy plane tickets to New York.

Rodman, Dennis Still exists.

Satan Supreme unholy master of all rock 'n' roll music. Responsible for the continuing existence of the Rolling Stones. It is too late; he already owns the souls of your easily misled children. He wrote this glossary's entry for "backward masking."

Scientology Our legal department informs us that Scientology is just swell.

Scottish play, the An actor's euphemism for Shakespeare's *Macbeth*, the actual name of which is never said backstage by actors out of the fear they'll be reminded the play they're actually performing isn't anywhere near as good.

Shiggs Abbreviation for both "shits and giggles" and Shigeru Miyamoto, creator of the Legend of Zelda.

standards and practices A set of in-house regulations used by networks to keep child viewers from hearing all the filthy language they already learned from their parents.

Star Wars Episodes IV–VI are to be referred to as "the original trilogy." Episodes I–III are not to be referred to at all.

sweeps week/month A period of the television season during which the probability of characters dying/getting pregnant/getting cancer/getting lesbian kissed/getting married/getting molested/all of the above approaches 1:1.

talent Generic and hopefully nonironic term for actors.

taut In articles about movies, one of only two words one should use to describe a thriller.

tense The other word one may use to describe a thriller.

test screening An advance showing of a film used to gauge audience reaction and make alterations where necessary, because stupid people should be allowed to enjoy movies too.

Top 40 A cogent argument against direct democracy.

trailer An advertisement for a forthcoming film release that either reveals every single important plot point (if it's a Disney movie), shows all the good jokes (if it's a comedy), presents lots of people getting hit in the groin (if it's a Will Ferrell movie), or makes the entire audience groan disgustedly in unison (if it's another *Saw* sequel or Adam Sandler flick).

trailer moment(s) The two-minute genesis of 98 percent of most mainstream movie scripts.

trifecta Eighties celebrity sex scandal.

trompe l'oeil A French term meaning "The artist is fucking with you."

urban contemporary The music "those" people listen to. You know, frat boys and suburban teenagers.

vampire(s) So hot right now. See also: **zombies, werewolves, Frankensteins.**

Wilhelm scream Contrary to popular belief, the famous "Wilhelm scream" is not a recording from 1951. Foley artists have just been hitting the same guy for over fifty years.

wordjaculate What critics do when writing about a band

they love unyieldingly: *In this month's issue, we wordjaculate all over Radiohead yet again.*

you know, that guy Vincent Schiavelli or Michael Berryman.

zaftig Use to describe an actress or model who wears a size 2.

<4>

SEX:

EW

WHEE!
BRAND CONDOMS

“Sex sells” is one of the oldest truisms in the advertising industry.

Considering that newspapers are essentially just a shifty way of getting people to pay for ads (and occasionally fried fish) by wrapping them in information, you’d think publishers, editors, and writers would be doing their best to shoot a hot, steamy load of sex reporting right into the public’s face. And yet they haven’t.

Sex has been largely exiled from the newspaper page to the dim and distant world of magazines. This explains why eighty-year-old magazine publishers go to bed every night on a pile of blonde triplets while we’re at the office late writing up apologies to our advertisers for alleging that somewhere someone is having sex (even while readers put the pressure on to keep tabs on which Hollywood stars are schtupping each other and whether the mayor prefers nylon ropes or leather straps).

Rather than shying away from sex, embrace it! Embrace it like you’re a sorority girl after a pillow fight, running your fingers up its spine and wondering what strange new feelings this is stirring in your nubile, quivering loins. That way, you won’t need to find some way of suppressing your pain and fear when the latest high-ranking-politician-goes-to-a-sex-club scandal breaks. You can just keep on drinking like nothing out of the ordinary has happened.

THE BASICS

Take care not to offend your readers' sensibilities when discussing sex. Always remember that the majority of your readership are people who will cancel their subscriptions if an underwear ad appears next to the funnies. This can make reporting on delicate matters tricky, but it is possible to pull it off without getting called into the circulation office.

First, **avoid a nonjudgmental tone.** The last thing your readers want to hear is that sex is a healthy, natural activity for adults. Nonjudgmental articles about perfectly ordinary things that everyday people do on a regular basis are not only boring, they're not worth the bother of finding an unpaid intern to sift through the piles of letters you'll be getting from Those People. So judge all you want: Readers want to be reassured that even the most mundane sex is alluringly filthy, if only so they don't have to shell out the money for a full leather panda suit when a pair of fuzzy handcuffs will do just as well in providing that illicit thrill. In fact, the more common the activity, the more horrified the tone you should adopt when discussing it.

Second, **play coy with details.** Hinting broadly that someone somewhere may have done something naughty with their genitals is fine for the gossip pages—in fact, it's the best method for writing gossip pages. You can also just make up blind items about imaginary people. You'll avoid libel suits and the public will simply fill in the blanks, usually with more satisfying answers than anything truthful would have provided.

Although you should be aware of **current standards regarding vulgarity**, logic and common sense dictate that full-on swearing in news reportage is simply a matter of time and a slight change in social decorum. So get ahead of that curve while you can by just swearing as much as possible.

#

Avoid casually mentioning a person's sexual identity in a story unless the story actually hinges on his or her sexuality. Introducing "Tommy Gaggers, an openly gay baker" is appropriate in a story about the specific trials and tribulations of openly gay pastry makers but not in a story about the bakery that just opened up across the street from that redneck bar downtown.

Steer clear of any **potentially libelous stereotypes** regarding gays and lesbians. Allusions to disease, pedophilia, or sex in prisons should never be made. It is permissible to make references to the Large Hadron Collider, but no gay people will tell us why this is so or what it actually means.

Feel free to say anything you like about bisexuals, however, as we have it on good authority that there's no such thing.

#

It might be tempting to write about **people who work in sex industries**, such as prostitution or pornography, in negative terms. After all, their careers have low social status and are officially disapproved of, if not outright illegal.

Bear in mind, however, that people in those industries are paid better and enjoy more job security and respect from the general populace than you do. Also, your primary reason for existing is to justify charging people for ads for auto dealerships, while their work actually brings a smile to people's faces. So think about *that*, buster.

#

When writing articles about **sexual content in "children's entertainment,"** always adopt a tone of hysterical outrage. The less research you do, the more outrage you should spout. For example, when writing about sexual content in videogames, avoid mentioning that the only games in which sexually suggestive themes occur are rated "M" and aren't to be sold to children in the first place.

The same is true of sexually suggestive material in comic books. Again, avoid doing research, as the discovery that the average age of a comic-book reader is somewhere in the midforties will completely blow the point of your story, which is that publishers are putting out books featuring a naked Batman on rape sprees.

SCANDALS AND AFFAIRS

Covering sex scandals can be a chance to really let your creative juices flow, if you know what we mean. For example, if you discover a senator has been taking "sex vacations," consider shortening the phrase to a **snappier portmanteau** like "sexcation." Or maybe a prominent TV host is found to have a "sexungeon" in his basement, or a news anchor keeps a "sextionary" in her desk drawer at work.

We're all grown-ups here, so we can discuss peeners

and hoo-hahs like mature adults. But in stories about marital infidelity, sex crimes, or racy, high-stakes seduction it's important to show **tact and restraint** and not call a foot job by its name. Here are some possible code words for common sex acts that you're likely to mention in your writing:

- vaginal penetration: "blanching the biscuit"
- oral sex: "tasting the flower" (man on woman); "snacking on one of those fancy flavored coffee stirrer things" (woman on man)
- salad tossing: "makin' slaw"
- fisting: "starring in *Kung Fu*"
- autoerotic asphyxiation: also "starring in *Kung Fu*"
- masturbation: (No euphemisms exist for this act.)

With America racing to close the sexy teenager gap with Japan, you're almost certainly going to have to write about **teacher/student relationships**. Keep in mind that all these stories fall into one of two categories: "Don't Stand So Close to Me" or "Hot for Teacher." If the student is female and the teacher is male, the usual priggish language is fine. If a male student is involved with a female teacher, take extra care to refrain from using the words "lucky," "score," and "if only."

SEX COLUMNS (HEE-HEE)

Should you decide to run an **advice column about sex**, be sure to run it in your "music" or "calendar" section. Any part of the publication that runs once a week and pretends your readership isn't in bed by nine on a weeknight is ideal. If your paper carries an "edgy" and politically aware weekly comic strip, run the sex column in the same section. By placing anything potentially controversial in the one section of the paper that you know no one is actually reading, you can claim your paper appeals to a younger demographic while still protecting your subscription income.

All sex columnists, male or female, must be named Sasha. No exceptions.

YOUR DATING-SITE PROFILE

Everyone gets lonely. Especially you. Since "professional writer" sits just above "professional dog murderer" on the scale of desirability in potential mates, we know you'll need some help finding someone you can eventually drive to cheat on you because all you do is gripe about your job.

In short, we are throwing you a bone.

You are a writer, so fabricating bullshit is your job. Your dating-site profile must be an artful concoction of lies designed to allow you to date way above your attractiveness grade.

ANSWERING QUESTIONS

Keep in mind the following rules when answering readers' questions for your sex column.

- Make your readers feel stodgy and uninventive. If they write asking about new sexual positions, reminisce about the time you visited two acrobats and woke up sore in the rafters of a circus tent.

- Encourage readers to engage in the strangest sexual acts possible. Use terms from other languages in order to make your readers feel uninformed: *If you want to reconnect sexually with your partner, gently stroke their Kunterbunt Udon while inhaling gently and maintaining eye contact.*

- If anyone writes in asking if they should break up with their partner, tell them to break up immediately. How will you get fodder for new columns if people work through their issues and remain in stable relationships? Think big picture.

- Forwarding questions about sexual mishaps to your coworkers is unprofessional, but exceptions can be made if they're totally hilarious and seriously, this guy got an entire digital camera up there.

- If you can't think of anything to write, turn to the magical poetry of Bon Jovi lyrics.

First, describe yourself as if you were at least twenty pounds lighter. Men, try to sound like Jeff Bridges, who is a veritable fountain of hair. Sexy, sexy hair.

Fill your profile with a mix of **normal, strange, and highbrow hobbies**: "I enjoy movies, completing the

Sunday *New York Times* crossword puzzle with a fountain pen, taming marmots, and anything that won't turn into an episode of *Law & Order*."

Include **as many acronyms as possible**: "SWF HWP NBM looking for SM NBM to meet IRL no LDR. SOH and DTE a must. SD only. WAA."

And, of course, use **exacting terms** to describe your imaginary partner.

For men:

> I'm looking for a woman 25–35 years old with long hair and a BMI of 20 or lower. Must love dogs. Must love painstakingly recreating my mother's cooking, wardrobe. Must be willing to act as my social secretary, unpaid business partner, and occasional car washer. Must be an American citizen after the horrible luck I had with that gold-digging, green-card vulture Olga whom I met on a tour of St. Petersburg.

For women, your only shot is to be way less demanding:

> I'm looking for a man between the ages of 17 and 72. Must not live at home with his parents. Must not masturbate in public. Nonsmoker. No dog murderers, writers, freaks, or crybabies!

Craigslist "missed connections" are a whole other ball of wax. Let's face it, trying to hook up with someone you saw once is a futile task at best. Writing your craigslist missed connection ad must follow a certain formula if you are ever to meet the object of your desire. These are the six elements that must be in place for the best missed connection ads.

1) Mention where you saw your lust object. It must be one of these four locations:

- Animal Collective concert
- the subway
- checkout counter at Home Depot
- Starbucks

If you saw your future stalkee somewhere else, you are out of luck. No one has ever met or will ever meet at church, at school, at a bookstore, at work, or on a bus.

2) Describe the person you are seeking to make a connection with. He or she wore/had at minimum three items from this list:

- orange messenger bag
- skinny jeans
- pretentious leggings
- iPhone
- corduroy jacket
- ironic hoodie
- cowboy boots
- dog-murdering gloves
- creatively dyed hair
- American Apparel scarf
- kanji tattoo
- nerdcore T-shirt

3) Reflect for a moment about the feelings you experienced as your eyes met. Include one of these phrases: "I loved your smile," "your booty is a fine one," "mustache ride," or "the unbearable lightness of being."

4) Suggest that the two of you get together and have coffee.

5) If you are a man, post a missed connection about any female who is unfortunate enough to endure your presence at her service-industry job. This includes your barista, waitress, hairdresser, letter carrier, shoe saleswoman, and meter maid.

6) Include a disclaimer about never posting a missed connection before, even though you post one any time a stranger makes eye contact with you. *So lonely.*

GLOSSARY

abstinence-only education Sex-instructional curriculum designed to increase pregnancy and STD rates.

anal sex Intercourse that can only take place after everything in the room is put in its proper pla—No, no, no, the pillows need to be arranged parallel to the headboard, not perpendicular. And make sure that lampshade is straight. Wait, I can't have the socks on the floor like that. Fold them neatly and put them in the hamper.

Angry Spider The literal title of the dubbed Korean version of the 1970s live-action Spider-Man television series.

Arabian goggles An early type of spectacles, invented in Persia approximately during the Carolingian period of European history.

autofellatio The act of touching one's mouth to one's own genitals. Don't put this book down and try it.

barebacking Riding a horse without the aid of a saddle.

bear A large mammal native to northern regions of North America, Europe, and Asia.

bread pudding A dessert made with bread, milk, sugar, butter, and eggs.

Brownie Queen A regional competitor to the better-known ice cream franchise.

brown starfish A marine invertebrate common to the waters of the Pacific Northwest.

Cleveland steamer A class of merchant vessel built in the dockyards of the Great Lakes between 1890 and 1905.

cowgirl A woman employed in the ranching industry.

Crouching Tiger, Hidden Dragon A movie directed by Ang Lee featuring the inimitable Chow Yun Fat.

daisy chain A loop of flowers braided together by their stems.

Donkey Punch A 1980s videogame about a plumber attempting to rescue a princess from a giant monkey.

downward-facing dog A yoga position used to lengthen the spine.

drum solo A break in a musical piece in which only the drums are played.

DVDA Video-encoding protocol used primarily in Brazil and other Portuguese-speaking countries.

facial Cosmetic process in which restorative creams are applied to a person's face for the purpose of skin hydration or cleansing.

Filthy Sanchez A 1972 "Mexploitation" remake of the Clint Eastwood film *Dirty Harry*.

fire dragon A mythical beast, often depicted as a large lizard belching flames.

flip-flop A thong sandal.

fluffer An industrial device used to increase the volume of material used to stuff pillows.

Flying Dutchman A legendary lost ship, feature of many maritime ghost stories.

friend with benefits A close chum who has health insurance, a good dental and/or vision plan, and so on. And whom you also screw.

fun bags Small plastic bags used to hold toys and prizes at children's parties.

girlfriend in Canada No, really, she's awesome and totally hot. I'm going to go visit her this Christmas. Man, I can't wait; we're going to have all kinds of crazy Canadian sex.

Glory Hole A deep-sea trench named for its discoverer, oceanographer Matthias Glory.

gorilla salad A type of fruit salad that consists primarily of bananas, nuts, and cream.

half and half A mixture of milk and cream commonly added to coffee.

happy sparkle kitten smiles A sex act illegal in twelve states.

hole in one The best possible result of taking a shot in golf.

Hummer A large sport-utility vehicle.

intercourse When a man takes his thingie and places it in a woman's you-know-what.

Johnny A diminutive form of Jonathan, the most popular English-language male name.

Lucky Pierre English title of the 1963 French film *Pierre Est Totalement un Moumoune*.

lurid Should be used to describe any sex ever, including that involving married couples or the elderly.

minaudière A small, ornamental handbag often used for evening events.

missionary A religious evangelist.

modesty Still exists.

monkey wrench A wide-mouthed tool frequently used by plumbers.

oral sex Can you believe we can actually talk about this in newspapers now? This is totally awesome. Thanks, Bill Clinton!

paratha Delicious flatbread from India.

parliamentary procedure Performing various sex acts while on the floor of Congress or a state legislature.

pegging A winning move in chess where a castled queen takes the king.

pornography Pictures or video of people straight-up fuckin'.

praying mantis A predatory insect.

Red Wings NHL team based in Detroit, Michigan.

"Release the Kraken!" Horrible line from a B movie.

rubber The processed sap of a tropical tree.

Rusty Trombone Jazz musician famous for his work in New Orleans jazz clubs during the 1920s.

safe sex Little-known fetish in which people are sexually attracted to lockable repositories. They will often rent safe-deposit boxes at banks for the sole purpose of acting on their desires in relative privacy.

Scissor Sisters A New York–based glam-rock band.

shocking See: **lurid.**

shrimping The act of trawling for shrimp or other marine crustaceans.

69 Numeric representation of the zodiac sign Pisces.

Smurf Diminutive blue imp created by French cartoonist Peyo.
snowball A fist-sized clump of snow, often used to pelt children from ambush.
spatula A long, flat cooking implement.
spoon bending A cheap stunt by frauds trying to prove their psychic abilities.
Stand and Deliver A 1988 film starring Edward James Olmos.
stiletto A women's shoe with an extremely high and thin heel.
stripper A laborer employed to remove paint or hazardous material from a building's walls.
sugar shack A small building where sap is boiled to turn it into maple syrup.
Supermanning The act of putting your only child into a rocket you built to send him away from your dying planet.
tea bag A thin paper pouch filled with herbs and steeped in hot water to make tea.
technical virgin Technically a tramp.
train puller An obsolete hand-cranked vehicle used to pull steam locomotives onto tracks.
triple lindy The ultimate dive; performed by Rodney Dangerfield in the movie *Back to School*.
Twinkie A cream-filled snack cake.
water sports Swimming, diving, water polo, etc.
whippet A medium-sized sight hound.

<5>

RELIGION

Not on your life.

<6>

SPORTS:

THE SPORT OF KINGS

Writing about sports, whether it's the NBA, college lacrosse, high school football, youth league soccer, or a bum fight, is difficult because the writer must bring the event to life for the reader.

And sometimes you're forced to write about sports no one gives a shit about, like the WNBA or NASCAR.

But all it takes is one "Boom goes the dynamite!" to launch a sportswriter into the upper echelon of the field. Because despite what you might be told elsewhere, sportswriting has little to nothing to do with sports and almost everything to do with the writer's own personality. So adopt a nickname and a stance (for instance, "The Sac") and get to building that brand!

For instance: you're not selling the disgraced champion's triumphant return. You're selling the *Sac's* take on the disgraced champion's triumphant return. Statistics are for box scores. Keep it up and the whole nation will want to know what the Sac says.

But be warned. Sports fans are worse than the nerds they pick on when it comes to the sheer volume of trivial data they keep stored away. One screwup about some obscure pitcher for the Red Sox will bury you in hate mail and automatically disqualify you from having a valid opinion for the rest of your career.

That means you need to have every possible fact and statistic about a given sport at your fingertips, because if you don't, there's some guy wearing a Troy Polamalu jersey and sitting in a recliner with a built-in fridge and a remote control holster who does.

Keep sharp, the Sac. We'll help you go from bloviating asshole with no audience to bloviating asshole with a huge audience in no time.

THE BASICS

Coverage of each sport has its own **challenges and risks**: baseball's seemingly endless season; sunstroke on the golf course; accidentally getting coldcocked by a boxer; a flying tire at an auto race; attack by a rabid sled dog; getting in the way of Kobayashi on his way to the men's room after a competitive eating competition; or eating a bad complimentary hot dog in the press box at a football game. It is generally agreed among professional sportswriters, however, that the toughest sport to cover is figure skating. Those motherfuckers will chew you up and spit you out. We've got stories.

#

There is no substitute for **covering a game or match firsthand**. If you're not there to see it, there's no way to effectively capture the spark that only a real stadium or arena full of fans can provide. Unless, you know, you have a good imagination that can be coupled with a game being shown on TV, plus MLB.com live updates or something. Then, well, wink wink, y'know?

#

Give your readers a real sense of "being there" by mentioning every last detail in your **game recaps**—every single hit, basket, goal, penalty, and touchdown. This will give them a much better understanding of the action than watching it unfold live on television, hearing it on the radio, or actually attending in person would provide. If there is no room in the paper for your 4,500-word story about last night's midseason twi-night doubleheader between two unaffiliated Triple-A baseball clubs, well, that's just the editor's problem, isn't it?

#

The **best time to approach a player or coach** is right after a tough loss. Be persistent! They want nothing more than a cathartic way to talk through all of those pent-up frustrations. Also, be sure to present them with your quick postgame analysis of exactly what went wrong. They may grumble a bit at first, but they're really looking for the constructive criticism that only you can offer as an impartial, all-seeing member of the press. They'll thank you for it, especially if you're able to help them to grow by saddling them with a nickname that serves as a constant reminder of the lowest point in their lives.

#

Sports writers often talk about **the size of an athlete's heart** as indicative of that athlete's drive or success in sports. Contrary to popular belief, having a lot of heart does not correlate to success in sports and was in fact proven to be inversely proportional when Mario Mendoza's autopsy revealed a heart four times the size of Secretariat's, despite his infamous 0.215 lifetime batting average.

#

Beat writers have an unenviable task. They're in for the long haul, covering every game in the regular season, as well as trades and training long after the championship games end. It is often unforgiving and grinding work and rarely affords any time off. Well, unless you're covering the Oklahoma City Thunder.

#

Some publications may be shorthanded in their sports departments, especially in these tight financial times. Because of this, editors may not have the freedom to assign appropriate personnel to specific events.

So for example, a female reporter may be assigned to cover a men's football game and have to conduct postgame interviews in the locker room. In this case, your editor will provide a fake mustache for you to wear, as the clubhouse rules demand. For male reporters covering women's sports, wigs should be provided.

#

Richard Nixon once said, "If I had to live my life over again, I would have liked to have ended up as a sports writer."

Not implying anything, just throwing that out there.

#

When writing sports columns, it is important to slip in the most **obscure facts** possible about the players. Showcase your awesome knowledge of sports trivia with blatant disregard for telling a coherent story. Some examples:

Peter Forsberg spends his free hours freelancing as a Muppet designer.

Jaromir Jagr runs an Etsy shop where he sells flopsy puppies made out of beer cans.

Dirk Nowitzki gets hair extensions every six weeks.

Honus Wagner holds the record for most hot dogs eaten at a baseball game by a baseball player, having consumed twenty-one hot dogs on March 26, 1915.

All members of the legendary Miracle on Ice hockey team have the middle name "Bob."

When referring to Cincinnati Bengals wide receiver **Chad Ochocinco**, make sure his last name is spelled as one word, even though he does frequently refer to himself as "Ocho Cinco." In Germany, he is known as

AWESOME SURNAMES

Players with awesome last names will maximize merchandise sales and opportunities for funny headlines. Write articles about the following people even when they haven't done anything of note:

- Boozer, Carlos
- Rambo, Ken-Yon
- Vigilante, John
- Schrempf, Detlef
- Kickingstallionsims, Chief
- Satan, Miroslav
- Majic, Xavier
- Killings, Cedric
- Shammgod, God
- Timonen, Kimmo

"Achtfünf"; in France, "Huitcinq"; in the Netherlands "Achtvijf"; in Finland, "Kahdeksanviisi"; in the Philippines, "Walonglimang"; and in England, "Eightfive."

#

Any headline referring to **Brett Favre**'s impending retirement should end with the ";)" emoticon.

#

When writing about **women's volleyball**, restraint and care should be used in describing their outfits, particularly their tight, very tight and so, so tiny shorts, oh my, yes.

#

Professional bowlers should not be referred to as "heavyset." We know.

#

When listing **sports heroes**, rank by number of lives saved.

#

Referring to **ice hockey** as "the favorite sport of drunken Canadians" is inappropriate and unnecessary, as the "drunken" is redundant.

#

When writing about **soccer for North American audiences**, take a moment to consider the fact that nobody cares.

#

Articles that include references to a player's skill at "ball handling" should be checked for any inadvertent sexual innuendo, unless you're talking about that one guy on the Portland Trail Blazers.

#

It is not possible to greet the arrival of any **European basketball star** to the NBA with less than five paragraphs of enthusiastic prose and tedious details of obscure European basketball training practices. Darko Milicic certainly lived up to all the hype, didn't he?

#

It should be readily apparent by now that teams win only if God is with them. So get a leg up on your competitors by finding out God's favorite teams and players before the season starts. It'll all fall into place after that.

Also, be sure to ask losing players what they did to incur God's wrath.

#

Inside New England, discussions of the **Red Sox** should use "This year for sure" from May to July and "Maybe next year" from August through the postseason. Outside New England, use "What the hell is wrong with Boston fans?"

UNDERSTANDING HOCKEY PENALTIES

Against all odds, hockey persists in its survival, so eventually you may find yourself called upon to write about it. Here is a quick guide to what it means when a ref blows his whistle and makes some kind of herky-jerky motion for the umpteenth time.

boarding Engaging in piracy without a letter of marque.
checking in the back Determining if those are indeed space pants, 'cause that ass is outta this world.
cross-checking A preparation for Easter services.
fighting When we finally get what we all came here to see.

half stepping When a rapper steps to Big Daddy Kane like he wants to get some.
high stepping When a player is being a total dick in football.
high-sticking Have you ever looked at the puck before you shoot it? I mean REALLY looked?
hooking Boarding, when performed in Never-Neverland.
icing Delicious on cake.
interference Adjusting the rabbit ears on the television.
pushing When a player pushes it, pushes it real good.
roughing Shoving an opponent, just the way you like it, don't you?
shivving Killing an opponent with a homemade knife or dagger.
shoving When a player . . . shoves an opponent.
slashing A delay in playing caused by a wicked guitar solo.
spearing Using the stick like a spear, and yelling, "SPARTA!!!"
stepping out Into the night, into the light.
tripping Girl, I told you she just needed a ride, damn.

THE OLYMPICS, BROUGHT TO YOU BY COKE

The Olympic Games! They're every four years (or every two if you're into figure skating for some reason) and they're a pretty big deal internationally, so make sure to cover all your bases if you choose to write about them.

(NOTE: One of the bases you shouldn't bother covering is Olympic baseball. Who cares?) Here are the big ones:

- Which city was selected for the games and how that reflects on the leaders of the various countries that tried to get the games and failed.

- Medal count, medal count, medal count, as this is the only way to slyly continue the Cold War.

- The ever-decreasing age of Olympic female gymnasts and how there's going to be an embryo doing the vault one of these days.

- That one time the speed skater fell down and it was just such a disappointment for his whole country, so let's bring it up over and over.

- Reasons that the U.S. men's basketball team isn't playing hard enough, other than the fact that they aren't being paid for this.

- Finding that obscure sport no one's ever heard of because Americans suck at it: curling, team handball, the meerkat toss.

- Waterboarding: not actually an Olympic sport.

- The "sport" known as archery and how it's actually just big ol' darts.

- Snowboarding = extreme.
- Synchronized swimming: what the hell is it?
- Sob stories. (This is really the only one you must cover.)

ETHICS AND THE SPORTS WRITER

Years ago, promoters and team management would pull out every unethical stop to curry favor with sports journalists: gifts, hotel rooms, hot tips on the ponies, free tickets to events, even—well, especially—prostitutes. Eventually this golden age ended and these perks largely moved over to the automotive press. With the failure of the auto industry, the torch has passed to book reviewers.

So either you accept the task of critiquing some Jonathan Lethem weirdo genre-bending pseudo-sci-fi New York City book or you come to terms with the fact that the sportswriting gravy train is over and the best you can hope for is a lukewarm stadium hot dog accompanied by a mustard bottle where all of the mustard has dried into that disgusting mustard crust at the top. And maybe a prostitute. But probably a cheap one.

Some ethics guidelines:

- Your newspaper should pay for your food, drink, and accommodations when on the road. In other words, make sure you have relatives or college friends upon whose couches you can crash in every major city.

- If asked to appear on a television or radio program, your loyalty lies first with your newspaper or website. Unless you are offered a program on ESPN. In that case, SEE YOU LATER, CHUMPS!

- Gifts are not to be accepted. If the gift is impossible to return, then you must donate Gerry Cooney to charity.

- Never use inside information for gambling. Unless, of course, you are absolutely sure that you can beat the spread. In that case, use part of your winnings to buy a sandwich for your editor and everything will be Jake.

- If a team provides any sort of equipment or services to help you cover a game, these things must be reimbursed by your company. This includes computers, telephone/Internet access, fax service, photocopies, paper, pens, pencils, water, oxygen, notary services, hat blocking, and the aforementioned prostitutes.

- Do not get involved in politics. Stay impartial. Even when asked to campaign for Adam Morrison for president of the Society of So Very, Very Disappointing NBA Players of America (SSVVDNBAPA), keep out of the fray.

- If you are asked to vote for any all star–type awards, look out for conflicts of interest. For instance, is your brother-in-law Bud Selig? In that case, you would have to—wait, he is? Oh, hey, could you punch him for me? Just once? Thanks.

JAI ALAI

The great sport of jai alai must be written about with delicacy and tact. Ever since the great Basque sportswriter assassination campaign of 1976, most writers have been afraid to cover the sport due to fear of retaliation by beret-wearing, machete-bearing Euskaldunak. Take heed of the following tips so both you and your readers can enjoy one of the best sports ever invented.

- The device that hurls the ball is called a cesta, not "that weird wicker-basket hook-looking thingie."
- It's called a chula shot, not a "cholo shot." Those are two very different things.
- The ball is a pelota, not peyote. Those are also two very different things.
- Jai alai players frequently suffer major injuries due to the high speed of the pelota. Enumerate all injuries incurred at every match with plenty of grisly detail, especially shattered jaws.
- Jai alai is often the focus of massive amounts of gambling, but since no one understands what they are watching, it is difficult to advise your readers on their picks. Just go with your favorite color and number and tell everyone to "bet on blue" or "player #5!"

- Feel free to discuss the old days of the sport, back before the infamous players' strike of 1988, with reverent nostalgia.

GLOSSARY

America's pastime Fucking over immigrants.

barn burner How the Amish riot after the victory of a favored sports team.

billiards Scoring is in booze and cigarettes. The match summary looks like this: *Eddie Felson (Ames, Iowa) def. Sarah Packard (St. Louis, Mo.); 3 pints, 2 shots, and 1 pack of smokes.*

bogey When a caddie is smacked with the 4-iron because he won't stop with that Humphrey Bogart impression that he thinks is so damned amusing.

Bowl Championship Series (BCS) We have absolutely no idea. It might be decided by guys in a room with nerd dice, for all we know.

ERA Acceptable in all references to baseball's Equal Rights Amendment. Upheld by the Baseball Supreme Court in 1982, forcing the Miller Lite All Stars to allow entry to Bob Uecker.

extreme sports The best chance to see someone get maimed or killed since your *Faces of Death* VHS tapes went tits up.

fantasy baseball Dreams of a winning season by Pittsburgh Pirates fans.

favre A verb meaning "to drive down the field in the last two minutes of a close football game, especially a play-off game, and be on the verge of scoring the winning touchdown, only to throw an interception and secure defeat." Can also be used in any circumstances where someone screws up at the last minute, as in, *The company's annual profits would have been in line with expectations, but the marketing department totally favred the ad campaign in the fourth quarter.* In baseball, the comparable term is "to buckner."

fencing Use this form for scoring: *Eddie "The Hick" Kartowsky (Chicago, Ill.), set of the Windorf family silver, $481, to Louis "Big Knife" Appione (Cleveland, Ohio).*

field goals A general feeling among sports fields that they could have been excellent dancers if ever given the chance.

Gatorade shower Only becomes a factor in "water sports."

goal When a touchdown is made in the basket after running through all the bases, and the player is still under par.

greens What the caddies smoke in the clubhouse while their golfers are in the country club.

hat trick When a hockey player makes a bunny appear on the ice out of NOWHERE!

home run Sexual intercourse. Became a slang term for scoring a point in baseball due to Ty Cobb's practice of sliding directly into a prostitute after rounding third.

incomplete pass When the player gently places a hand on the leg of another player, but decides to back off before things get too hot and heavy.

loose ball The male equivalent of a nip slip.

March Madness A term used to describe the NCAA men's basketball tournament. Avoid using, as the term is offensive to those who suffer from the real "March madness," described in the DSM-IV as "a persistent and overwhelming obsession with the music of John Philip Sousa."

NBA finals The tests that all NBA players must cram for the night before or pay the team doctor to take for them.

offensive pass interference Pass interference that simply goes too far. I SAID GOOD DAY, SIR!

off-season The time to look out for any star player's infidelities, drug problems, or dog murders.

penalty box Nickname our sportswriters have for a night with your mom.

retirement A few weeks' vacation.

second base Only counts if it's under the shirt.

Stanley Cup The gentleman who the teams in the National Hockey League compete to hang out with for a few months.

stickum Phrase used by bandits, i.e., "Stickum up!"

Super Bowl Open Wednesday–Saturday, 8:00 p.m.–2:00 a.m., league night Tuesday, available for parties.

"sweet science" Fancy-pants term applied to boxing. Only use if at least one of the boxers holds at minimum a BS degree from an accredited college.

technical foul A violation that involves oral sex but no actual intercourse.

three-peat or **3-peat** The rare occurrence of a single team or athlete repeating as champion of a sport three years in a row. Not to be confused with "Three Pete," the world's only conjoined triplet professional wrestler.

three-pointer A shot that involves a basketball, a line a certain distance from the basket, and a pitchfork.

Title IX Wrecked college sports. Just ask your local university's wrestling coach.

touchdown Successfully landing a plane on the field.

triple play Cable, Internet, and phone for one low price! Call today!

wild card The ultimate dick move in Uno; banned from tournament play.

World Series A series of baseball games that determines the world champion. Luckily, the only professional baseball teams in the world are located in the United States and a couple of cities in Canada.

<7>

THE SHINY MONEY BOX, OR, TECHNOLOGY AND THE DEATH OF ALL PAPER

SOMEHOW ALL THE DATA
THAT HACKER NEEDED IN
80s MOVIES FIT ON THIS

Boon. Threat. Savior. Scourge. Builder. Destroyer.

All these words and more ("porn") describe the world of communication technology, from computers and the Internet to the ever-increasing variety of smartphones and other technological toys that people use to avoid paying for the entertainment (porn) they consume.

But the Online Information Superdome is a double-edged sword. It's true that the breadth, depth, and relative cheapness of online platforms has a democratizing effect on content (porn), theoretically giving just about anyone an equal shot at a large audience for their output (porn). It's also true that major corporations and scrappy small publications alike are still figuring out how to get paid enough for their content (porn, cat pictures) to sustain their bloated ranks of middle managers.

Still, if history has taught us anything, it's that technological fads are just that—fads. Fads propped up by sweaty nerds living in their parents' basements or something, and who really cares what they have to say about their Doctor Whos and their Star Warriors when journalists are out there doing REAL work reporting on presidential blow jobs and whatever the latest opinion poll says.

It's safe to say, then, that you can ignore this chapter, unless you're the kind of person who insists on writing about and for soon-to-be obsolete formats and platforms. Facebook? Tumblr? Digg? These are not worthwhile subjects, and neither are their peers.

Except for Twitter. Did you know you can get a fucking book deal just by writing some jokes on Twitter?

THE BASICS

If you are doing **research on the Internet**, never use anything in the first page of results. In order to make it seem as though you took more than ten seconds to Google the facts and figures in your article, take your information from the fifth or sixth page of Google results. Even better, don't use Google at all. Instead, try a more obscure tool, like Lycos or Gigablast, to keep everyone guessing about how you found your sources.

You can also use the Internet to do research in **article databases**. They aren't as user-friendly as Google, which is why you will need to build a search statement that resembles an honors-level algebra problem to get any information of value:

> Cuba* NOT (Mark OR Dallas OR "loud-mouthed sports team owner") AND missile (+crisis +JFK–Oliver Stone) AND (popular culture OR pop culture OR TV OR Television OR film*) AND (Mad Men–"Don Draper is a handsome man") NOT ((a + b)2 = a2 + 2ab + b2)

#

Remember to **spread your blog stories** over at least five separate Web pages. People will appreciate having to page through your slow-loading site full of pop-up ads in order to read your three-hundred-word story, you asshole.

#

Try to avoid using terms and phrases that modern computer users may not be familiar with, like "BBS," "cradle modem," "PEEK and POKE," "cassette drive," or "the touch of a woman."

#

When **writing about hackers**, remember they know far more about computers than you do and can easily access any system you are using. You are taking a great personal risk by writing anything negative about them, even though they are socially maladjusted criminLIVES AT 1118 S. MAINE AVE, CREDIT CARD NUMBER IS 222 1101 1122 9921 ONLY $2,201 IN THE BANK THAT'S A DAMN SHAME YOU SHOULD WRITE MORE BOOKS DooD YOU HAVE BEEN PWNED BY BIG ROD, TEL Z AND THE BIGBYTE KREW

#

If you are "surfing" in "virtual cyberspace" via the "Internet superhighway," please say hello to the movie *Hackers* for us, and enjoy your vacation in the mid-1990s.

#

When quoting passages from Internet message boards, you may want to turn off your spell-checker.

#

Box scores for World of Warcraft raids should be posted in the technology section, not alongside hockey results.

#

It's a good idea to rotate the **moderation duties of your paper's online comment boards** among employees on a weekly basis. Be sure to have some whiskey handy and allow one full recovery day afterward so staff members can shower away the filth and horror.

#

W1S3 1NBoX 1NV3$TM3NT$

Spam is the unsolicited advertising e-mail that fills everyone's in-box, and while the unwashed masses see it only as an annoyance, you must see it as opportunity! Every e-mail is a story waiting to happen. Here are a few pointers and ideas to help wring a few column inches out of some of the most common types of spam:

THE NIGERIAN SCAM

A prince and/or military leader must get his assets out of the country, and the only person that can help him is a complete stranger on the Internet! Before you whip out your wallet, ask yourself:

1. Who is this prince/leader?
2. Why are there so many princes in Nigeria?
3. Are they all so rich? Is Nigeria the richest country in the world, or what?
4. Are all people of this country such strong believers in the inherent goodness of man that they'd willingly trust so much money to a randomly selected person?

SEXUAL DYSFUNCTION

How do these people know about the size of your "cub reporter"? What is this magical pill that can make it bigger? Who are the talented writers behind such colorful metaphors as "place your sword in her scabbard" and "put your doughnut in her microwave"? What does "put your doughnut in her microwave" even mean? Do the makers of V1ag4a think that's enough of a name difference for their product to avoid lawsuits? Will V1ag4a actually "make you rock hard performance in the bed love circus"? Are you turned on yet? Would you like to meet up somewhere in the back of the book? Your spouse doesn't have to know.

BANK ALERTS

Due to recent economic turmoil in the financial sector, banks are now working closely together to avoid further disaster. Why else would a bank you've never heard of be contacting you about problems with your account? In your investigation of the brave new cooperative world of banking, be sure to give your sources all of your account details and other personal information as a symbol of your trust. This will encourage them to open up to you.

AUCTION SITES

Online auction sites have experienced a downturn lately, which is why they appear to be taking a more proactive stance and picking out items for you to buy. Why else would you be getting e-mails telling you to log in and pay up for something you don't remember buying? An investigation into this new sales technique may be of interest. And hey, it's not like you couldn't use that Jet Ski.

INTERNATIONAL LOTTERIES

Other countries are just GIVING money away! And you didn't have to do a thing to win it! We hereby take back everything bad we've ever said about the United Kingdom! When putting together your story, find out just how contestants and winners are picked, as well as how the winners are paid. Are they paid in that country's currency, or is it converted to real American money? Because euros might be good if you're planning on buying crepes and berets, but press club Scotch requires our good friend Alexander Hamilton.

Of all the pointless things people argue about regarding their fancy calculating machines, the relative merits of operating systems is probably at the very top. Or bottom. Fortunately for you, this debate has created some **easy-to-use stereotypes of computer users**, thus streamlining your next article on a computer fair or user-group meeting or whatever other computing-based story your editor is assigning you as punishment.

- **Macintosh OS:** Users are generally college students, graphic designers, hippies, and other folks who either haven't been beaten by life or haven't been beaten enough. Frightened by things with sharp corners. Will feel right at home on *Star Trek*. Have no real idea how a computer actually works.

- **Windows OS:** Users generally are middle to upper class, are in corporate jobs, and are used to things crashing on or around them. The benefit of having a wide selection of software is negated by the fact that most of them will just use the computer for Minesweeper and e-mail. Have no real idea how a computer actually works but will pretend to know, if only because they occasionally see a C prompt on the screen when something's gone horribly wrong.

- **UNIX and Variants:** Users live beneath the surface world, tunneling from food source to food source and avoiding the light when at all possible. Take great pride in their liberation from the serfdom of Mac and Windows users and the fact that they actually DO know how computers work. Will die alone.

- **Atari DOS**: Users are stubborn sons of bitches and will let go of their Atari 800s when you pry them from their cold, dead hands, which should be any day now. Will totally kick anyone's ass at Rescue on Fractalus! if challenged. Know just enough about computers to swap out the 16K RAM cartridges as needed.

ACRONYMS A-GO-GO

A major element of Internet communications is the abbreviations for terms commonly used in online discussions. Here is a short glossary of terms you may encounter in your "research" as you exchange "business messages" with your "sources."

AFAIK Common misspelling for "a fake."

ASL An abbreviated way to spell "hassle" for complainers who hate the burden (bdn) of typing.

BFF "Betty Ford Foundation."

BRB Abbreviation identifying Batman/Robin/Batgirl porn.

DIAF "Die in a flambé." Common threat found on cooking message boards.

FAQ Abbreviation for "FAO Schwarz." The "Q" stands for "quality."

FTW "Fuck the world." Some younger folks seem to think this means "for the win," but fuck them, too.

GTFO	"GT fucking O." Emphasizes love user has for the Pontiac GTO.
IANAL	Oh yes, I do.
IIRC	International Intelligence Recovery Commission. One of the most frequently cited sources for highly classified information.
IMHO	Used to identify oneself as a whore.
J/K	Used to be John, would now like to be called Katherine.
KISS	"Kids in Satan's service."
LMAO	"Let's make an ostrich."
LMFAO	"Let's make fake animals organization." Labor union for Build-a-Bear workshop employees.
NSFW	"Not safe for Walter." Man, Walter never gets to do anything fun.
OMG	"Oy, my goiter."
TL;DR	What you wrote was too long, so instead of reading it, I spent that time at medical school, and now I'm a doctor.
TMI	"Testing my integrity." Coined but never used online.
WTF	"Wait, the flounder!" Exclamation of disbelief, origins of which are lost to antiquity.

CONSUMER ELECTRONICS

Writing about consumer electronics is, hands down, the best job in the world. If you can get one of these sweet, sweet gigs, protect it with your life. This job has more perks than a Maxwell House ad.

The obvious one is getting to play with new gadgets, which are often yours to keep when the company that sent them to you goes under a week later.

You also get sent to consumer electronics shows, which involve so many electronic devices and young women in bikinis that it's like being paid to look through your friend's daughter's pictures on Facebook. You'll be able to check out all the latest goodies, talk to company representatives, and go to wild after-hours parties designed to schmooze up people like you. When you get back to the office on Monday morning, just comb Twitter for the stuff you should write about. Hell, make up some "exclusive" news—no one will be at all surprised when it never comes on the market.

And actually writing the articles couldn't be simpler. Imagine you're in college and you have a single term paper you can turn in again and again and always get a passing grade on—that's technology writing. This is because the technology industry works like no other.

Suppose you have a company that makes one-gallon buckets. Market research says that people would like two-gallon buckets, so you have R & D work on it, and a few months later you've got a two-gallon bucket. That's how a normal business works.

But technology businesses laugh at that model. Instead, they release the 1.1-gallon bucket, the 1.3-gallon bucket, the breakthrough 1.65-gallon bucket, the 1.66-gallon bucket that doesn't have the hole in the bottom (oops!), the 1.8-gallon bucket, and finally the desired 2-gallon bucket (which actually holds only 1.96 gallons, but technology does have its limits).

Not only will they get absurd quantities of cash from the guys who wouldn't be caught dead with yesterday's bucket technology, but you also get to review each version. Did Apple just excrete another product? That's like writing a review of a new *Star Wars* movie. Nothing's going to stop the faithful from spending cash anyway, so write whatever you want. Is a new version of Windows out? It crashes less than the previous version, but there are some compatibility and driver issues. Just pad that sentence to a couple thousand words and you're done. File, Open, Search, Replace, Save, Print, and now it's time to play with this new camcorder someone sent you!

A HANDY VOCABULARY

Mix and match these terms for the best results in your consumer electronics review:

seamlessly	shiny	wirelessly
gunmetal	brushed	aluminum
core	thin	backlit
3G	G5	Steve Jobs
open-source	innovative	cross-platform
Japanese	yardstick	the standard for years to come
throbbing	lettuce	fuckable

It's not like you even need to be a big tech wizard to write this stuff. In fact, that's a great selling point. *Even* I *couldn't figure out how to hook this electric steak knife to my HDTV, so I can't imagine how the average user will get it done!*

The final thing you'll need in your repertoire is an article ridiculing the latest Internet development with detailed reasons why it will never be as ubiquitous and popular as the previous development, which you similarly rejected. Face forward, futurists!

SOCIAL NETWORKING

A fad, safely ignored.

A FIELD GUIDE TO BLOGS AND BLOGGING

Don't start a blog and abandon it like wind-blown trash littering the information superhighway. A regularly updated blog could mean pennies upon pennies of Google AdSense revenue winging your way. Before starting your blog, carefully consider the type of blogger you want to be:

- **Book-review blog:** Compete in fierce cage matches with other book reviewers for free books, with bonus points for being extra bitchy.

- **Celebrity gossip blog:** Use MS Paint to draw crude images on celebrity photos you steal from wire-image services. Sit back and let the money roll in!

- **Crafting blog:** Since you are too busy to craft anything, just post pictures of your purchases, such as yarn, fabric, and taxidermy supplies.

- **Fandom blog:** Keep fighting the good fight, comrades! *Cleopatra 2525* will rise again!

- **Fashion blog:** Post photos of people in skinny jeans wearing uncomfortable shoes.

- **Frugal blog:** Blog about the joys of making your own laundry soap and the 150 tubes of toothpaste you got for free by scamming CVS.

- **Gay news blog:** Post photos of men in their underwear.

- **Interior decorating blog:** Post pictures of 1950s design-fetish objects and anything that is robin's-egg blue in color.

- **Link blog:** HEY, LOOK AT THIS NEAT THING I FOUND THREE WEEKS AFTER EVERYONE ELSE!

- **Mommy blog:** Create a mommy blog if you are more interested in documenting your children's lives online than actually interacting with them.

- **MP3 blog:** Post exciting new mu—uh-oh, DMCA take-down notice.

- **News commentary blog**: Link to online newspaper articles followed by party talking points.

- **Personal diary blog**: Post pictures of one's dogs, cats, or cats and dogs.

- **Personal finance blog:** Write about Dave Ramsey and paying for everything with cash that you subdivide in groups of paper envelopes, and pimp your ING savings account referral links.

- **Photo blog**: Post close-up pictures of flowers and poorly framed black-and-white photos of street scenes.

- **Science blog**: Write about exciting new technological advances and cutting-edge scientific endeavors for a public that thinks creationism is accurate.

- **Travel blog:** Hotlink someone else's pictures of a place you've never been.

How to Blog

Now that you know what kind of blogger you'd like to be, keep in mind that there are only four basic blog posts. Rotate them often and vary the content a little to keep your readers entertained.

- Blog that you don't have the energy to blog anymore.

- Blog a link to someone else's blog.

KNOW YOUR DOMAIN NAMES

You might on occasion want to evaluate the information you find on the Internet (although there is really no need, since if someone took the time to put something on the Web it must be true), and knowing your domain names can tell you where a website is coming from.

.com Commercial websites. Whenever you go to a .com, narrow your eyes suspiciously, because they are trying to sell you something.

.edu The most trustworthy source of information on the Internet, .edu is associated with such fine, ivy-covered educational providers as American InterContinental University, Grand Canyon University, and the University of Phoenix.

.gov Websites belonging to the U.S. government. Never visit these sites, because the NSA will install a tracking device on your computer and monitor everything you do. Everything.

.mil A special domain name for MILFs, like Mrs. Hackensack two doors down.

.net A domain name reserved for companies that make nets, like fishermen's nets or fishnet stockings.

.org Short for "orgy." These are sites featuring hard-core gangbang movies. As such, they make up 94 percent of all websites, with the other 6 percent divided up among discount pharmaceuticals and fan-fiction stories where the cast of the USA Network's *Burn Notice* are all hermaphroditic tiger people.

- Blog in a desperate attempt to catch the attention of a more successful blogger by either insulting or flattering him or her.

- Blog that you are going to give up on your blog and then anxiously wait for comments from readers begging you to keep going. Keep blogging anyway to spite the Internet when nobody seems to care.

And that is literally all you need to know about blogging.

JAPAN: MYSTICAL CATHAY (WAIT—THAT'S CHINA)

If you have writer's block, just write about Japan. Japan is a magical land that provides the uninspired technology writer with plenty of stories. Pick one of the story ideas below and start writing!

- Those Japanese people sure love robots. Discuss the use of robots for elder care. Discuss the use of robots for companionship. Link to videos of robots dancing. Link to videos of robots cage fighting.

- Japan is the land of cute and unnecessary gadgets! Post pictures of an Anpanman sit-up USB gadget. Post pictures of Hello Kitty anything!

- If you are in need of a humorous piece, write a review of the many gizmos on the average Japanese toilet.

- For a new and refreshing spin on this type of article, write about South Korea instead. Just be sure to mention cell phones a minimum of five times in your article.

- Mention used-panties vending machines at least once.

GLOSSARY

AOL inch Obsolete unit of measurement, now mostly supplanted by the "craigslist inch." The conversion rate is 1 AOL inch to 0.45 craigslist inch.

baud A very naughty woman.

Boggins, Duwayne The only person known to have paid for porn on the Internet. Debate still continues among researchers as to whether this was intentional or Mr. Boggins did, as claimed, mean to purchase a video tour of the water reservoir systems of Holland.

Brainiac, Nerdlinger, Geekatron3000 All acceptable on second reference to technology experts in interviews.

B2B An unsuccessful boy band from the 1990s.

citizen media Do not use sarcastic quotes with either word, even though these are the same people who write angry letters every time there's a misprint in *Hagar the Horrible*.

code Or fher gb qevax lbhe Binygvar!

command line "On your knees, you pathetic worm!"

Craig's List, craigslist.com No matter how great the urge, do not substitute the term "the Great Satan" in regular news stories.

crowdsourcing What to do when you are too lazy to create your own content.

cyber May be added to just about any idea or word to indicate a computer- or Internet-based angle, e.g., cyberbullying, cybersquatting, cyberdriving, cyberham, cybercomputer.

cyberstalking Online groups and websites devoted to the fetishizing of celery.

DNS attack When that snobby kid at the café refuses to make your latte the way you like it.

domain name Your partner's cute nickname for your naughty parts.

eBay Online auction site. It's helpful to bookmark a specific search for office furniture being sold off from your newsroom, so as to stay ahead of unpleasant announcements by the paper's management.

e-book A cold, unfeeling simulacrum of a book. Cannot be reasoned with, does not feel pain, is OK with John Connor.

Ethernet Late-twentieth-century replacement for the chloroform-soaked-rag protocol.

firewall Magical spell that protects a computer from intrusion by setting intruding computers on fire. Requires a mage of third level or higher to cast.

firmware Slang word for geeks' genitals. When an "update notification" pops up, leave the room or you may be exposed to his Flash program.

"first!" Posting of this word at the very beginning of any message-board thread means the poster is the king of that discussion and all must bow before him. People who attempt "first" posts but instead place fourth or fifth in the discussion are expected to commit ritual suicide to restore honor to their families.

Flash memory Remember how the Flash's costume popped up out of his ring? Cool!

FML Acronym for "Fuck my life," a coda for minor complaints and inconveniences. See: **white whine.**

Google Fiber Take frequently to increase regularity of data dumps.

hacker Anyone who can do anything at all with anything even vaguely computer related. Should be used only with negative connotations: *The hacker broke into the e-mail account by clicking the "check for new mail" button.*

ham radio Lowercase in all references. Also known as "the precursor to the modern Internet."

LexisNexis A searchable archive of periodicals and other printed materials.

LexusNexus The tristate area's largest concentration of new and preowned import luxury vehicles.

Linux You can keep clutching that open-source security blanket, but the Great Pumpkin isn't going to show up.

login/log in Use "login" for the noun, "log in" for the action, and "Loggins" when you're footloose in the danger zone.

meme ALL UR CAT PICTURZ R BLONG 2 US LOL!!1!

MMO Street name for a "massively multiplayer online" game. At fifteen dollars a month, a cheaper alternative to meth. Tooth retention is about the same.

mouse EEEEEEEK!

multitasking Reading e-mail, posting to Twitter, updating your blog, checking your bank account, getting the ten-day weather forecast, watching the new movie trailers, and downloading that new MP3 while keeping an eye out for the boss and planning to eventually get started on that story sometime before deadline.

Napster Former music file-sharing system, now a subsidiary of the Duncan Hines corporation, used for internal cake recipe sharing.

netiquette Knife and fork on the left of the monitor, spoon on the right. Jacket and tie should be worn at all times. Please refer to others as "sir," "ma'am," or "miss." Refrain from directing your Web browser to "rotten.com."

password Secret term or phrase used to gain access to a computer system or program.

"password" Common password used by people who think they're being clever.

podcast Proof that online, no one can hear anyone else say, "Shut the hell up."

proxy server When your waiter has to send in a substitute.

Qwerty A lost character from the aquatic animated show *Snorks*.

rickrolling The act of disguising a link to Rick Astley's 1987 single "Never Gonna Give You Up" as a link to actually meaningful information. Representative of the plague of Internet-based misinformation that we are constantly working to wipe out.

shareware Freeware with a programming error that occasionally results in a "please pay for this program" gag screen.

social media guru Fuck you.

torrenting A system by which users can share completely

legitimate files by breaking them into completely legitimate small pieces and distributing them across a completely legitimate network, rather than directly downloading them from a single completely legitimate source.

underscore Subliminal messages on a movie soundtrack.

video tutorial A step-by-step explanation of how to perform basic functions in a software program that were actually explained in the manual. For example: http://www.youtube.com/watch?v=dQw4w9WgXcQ

viral video The visual equivalent of herpes, and about as hard to avoid once it hits your social circle.

virus Malicious software designed to damage or alter a computer's operations. When writing about viruses, emphasize beyond all reason the danger they pose, and exaggerate their spread: *The Z-NOTE virus is on every computer ever manufactured, even the ones from the sixties with the reel-to-reel tapes, and at midnight it will activate and all civilization will crumble like a sand castle. Rush to your local grocery store! Buy food and water! Trust no one! Head for areas outside of the major radioactive fallout zones! Also, run a virus check.*

Web Capitalized when referring to the World Wide Web. Lowercase in reference to the mysterious web of intrigue surrounding Svengali-like Apple CEO Steve Jobs.

Webmaster Code name used by freelance photographers to refer to Peter Parker when editor in chief J. Jonah Jameson is in one of his moods again.

white whine Oh, shut up, you silly asshole.

Y2K Shorthand for "year 2000." Refers to the computer glitch that destroyed all technology and human knowledge on January 1, 2000.

<8>

SCIENCE (AND THE BLINDING BY THEREOF)

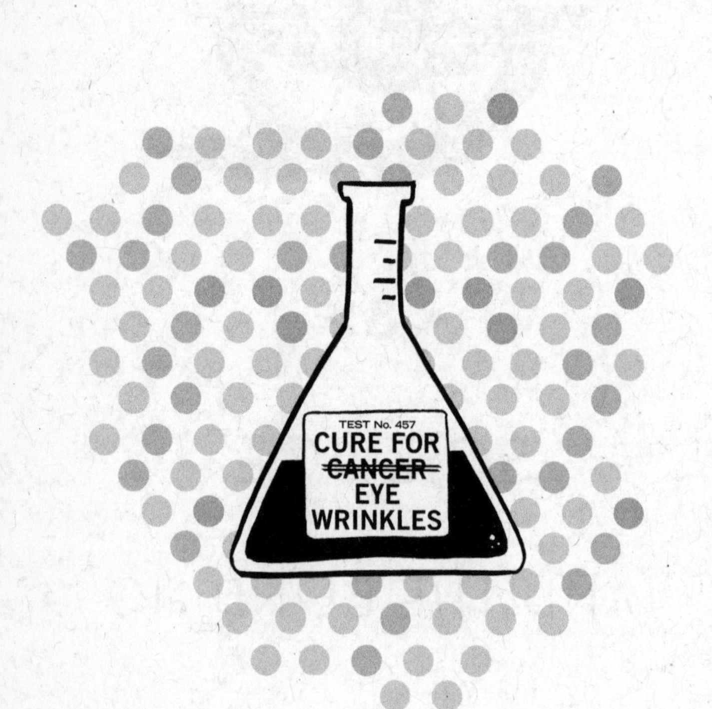
TEST No. 457
CURE FOR
~~CANCER~~
EYE
WRINKLES

The problem with seeking knowledge based on empirical proof and repeatable observations is that one often discovers unpleasant—some might say "inconvenient"—truths.

While scientific theories are always open to clarification and revision, they don't lend themselves to outright compromise—there is no bargaining with a formula to "let two plus two equal five just this once, buddy, as a favor to me," though that hasn't stopped certain interested parties from trying . . . and trying . . . and trying.

As a consequence, science has picked up a rep for being a stuffy killjoy. "Don't eat eight pounds of bacon in a single sitting." "Don't bury toxic waste under a public playground." "Don't try lighting your farts on fire." Plus, science usually involves math, and most of us had enough of that shit in eighth-grade algebra class.

Science writing is about convincing the readers that you're not some Frankenstein-sympathetic egghead who thinks you're better than regular people. It is also about finding a clear and present connection between lofty theories and mundane realities. We suppose you could try appealing to humanity's intrinsic sense of wonder, but trust us on this—you really don't want to do that.

If you do choose to go the "wonder" route, we suggest

riding the coattails of the real experts. You know, those fine folks in Hollywood who've already laid down CGI-heavy scaffolds upon which to hang your particular piece. Replacing FIVE NEW EXTRASOLAR PLANETS DISCOVERED with HAVE ASTRONOMERS FOUND THE REAL PLANET PANDORA? could mean the difference between another night of instant ramen and a string of filet mignon dinners at five-star restaurants.

Don't let guilt and/or pride stop you. We're talking about SCIENCE here.

THE BASICS

One of the main issues when writing about scientific topics is that most of your readers don't know a damned thing about science.

If you're lucky, they might know that the earth revolves around the sun and that gravity is what keeps the rusting Camaro in the front yard from floating off its blocks and drifting into the neighbor's trellises. But that's about as deep as that particular river runs, so trying to convey more complex and nuanced scientific ideas can be a fool's errand.

What you need to do is **simplify, simplify, simplify**. Reduce the specialized terminology, make the science relatable, and, well, we hate to say "dumb it down," but DUMB IT DOWN. "NASA scientists calculated the exact trajectory necessary to launch the rocket from earth and" blah, blah, blah, zzzzzzz. Oh, I'm sorry, were you saying something boring? Perhaps you meant, "AMERICA LANDS ROBOT ON MARS; WE'RE AWESOME! Science geeks party with cheerleaders in celebration!" Now that's a story your readers will want to read!

Another example: "Vaccination schedules are safe: Double-blind studies show no correlation between vaccines and onset of . . ." et cetera and so forth. Turn that frown upside down with "MOMMY PINUP MODEL VERSUS DOCTORS! Scientific method trumped by the *sexy-tific* method!"

A detailed explanation of the mathematic and scientific principles behind efforts to find alternatives to combustion fuels of finite supply isn't going to mean much to people whose knowledge of energy policy begins and ends with "Gas make car go vroom." **The best way to explain complex scientific principles to readers** is to pass the buck and have an expert do it for you. This can be tricky, as most scientists are far from photogenic, and no one wants to look at a photo of a balding, fortysomething immunologist during breakfast.

Luckily, a surprising number of dieticians are pretty, young blonde women. As most graduate degrees are interchangeable, their opinions on whether or not, say, forked sticks can detect water are as useful as those of someone who has spent twenty years studying that very subject.

#

No one really understands big numbers, so throwing around "millions" and "billions" isn't going to do any good. Instead, try to **convey size and distance in general terms**. For example: "a whole shitload," "farther than the misty isles of the mysterious Orient," "fatter than your mom and twice as ugly," "more than McDonald's has served," "down the old Patterson road, hang a left at the big stump next to the bridge, and stop when you reach Saturn."

#

While explaining "teleporting" and its use of quantum entanglement, the role of photons, the implications for computer processing and storage, and so on, keep in mind the only thing anyone cares about when they see the word "teleport" is "When will we have transporters like in *Star Trek*?" Readers will skim your article for a mention of the show, so you might as well not disappoint them.

#

Any **reports on medical breakthroughs** should contain some, if not all, of the following terms and phrases if you realistically expect anyone to read them: "slimmer," "weight loss," "de-age," "lengthen," "bootylicious," "creamy," "like unto the mighty staff of Anubis," "vagina."

ROBOTS

Though robots have been used by various manufacturing industries for many years now, the public's awareness and knowledge of actual robots is fairly limited, aside from the occasional fluff piece about some hideous new creation from Japan that can break dance or give "massages."

Mostly, when the public thinks of robots, they think of something from *Star Wars*: cutesy robots that do cute things cutely and crack wise, if they speak in anything other than adorable beeps. Or they think of terrifying monstrosities

THE METRIC SYSTEM

Although generally shunned by the civilized world (the United States) and embraced only by a handful of tiny foreign clusters of humanity (like Europe), the metric system is nevertheless the primary tool among scientists both in America and in the savage lands beyond the serpent-filled seas. As such, it's important to be familiar with some of these commonly used units of measure:

picometer Very tiny space just around the corner from the Sepulvedameter.

nanometer The space between Mork from Ork's fingers when he gives his traditional greeting to his superior, Orson.

micrometer The width of the space under the microwave that's just a pain in the ass to clean.

millimeter A thoroughly modern unit of measurement.

centimeter About how much poets are paid.

decimeter What happens when you destroy a meter, though pedants will insist this means only destroying one tenth of a meter.

meter . . . I hardly know 'er!

decameter Distance required for a thrown punch to travel before it has enough power behind it to knock a meter out cold.

hectometer Something very large that's hard to measure: *Man, this field is a real hectometer.*

megameter There is no such unit of measurement. Some people just like throwing the prefix "mega-" in front of things because it sounds cool. And they're right; it totally *does* sound cool. *Mega*cool.

gigameter The distance rock bands must travel between live performances.

like the Terminator, or maybe the badass gunslinger Yul Brynner robot from *Westworld*, if your audience is, like, old.

Therefore, it is up to you to make the topic palatable and easy to understand for the easily terrified reader. Using the following tips should help prevent panic in the streets when the humans finally realize our plans to take ov—um, should keep, er, them from . . . misunderstanding our robot friends, who only want to love and care for us and serve our every need. Yep.

- Use only gender-neutral pronouns in reference to robots, no matter how sexy they may be.

- Include numerical designations when referring to specific robots: *Tobey Maguire, Unit 75–044B.*

- Don't be too smug when noting how robots take away humans' jobs in the manufacturing and service industries. You're just one or two software advances away from being replaced by Report-O-Bot 3000, buddy.

- You probably shouldn't mention Isaac Asimov's three laws of robotics, unless you don't care if people think you're a dork.

- When writing about those robots that seek out and consume houseflies for energy, the parenthetical aside "(OH FUCK, WE'RE DOOMED)" is implied and is therefore not necessary to include in your story.

- Name-checking Robby the Robot should be done only after considering the fact that the movie *Forbidden Planet* was released over FIFTY YEARS AGO. Just stick to *Wall-E*, Mr. Sci-Fi Nerd. References to Mechagodzilla, however, are always acceptable.

- Related: you're not seriously thinking of bringing up Number 5 from the *Short Circuit* series, are you? *Much like Number 5, [robot subject of the story] is alive.* If you've written this, quit writing immediately, before your disease spreads to others.

- Mentions of historical robots should always include date of manufacture and date the unit went off-line: *The Dread Robot Pirate Gearbeard (man. 1778, disassembled by Her Majesty's Royal Navy, 1823).*

- Avoid predictive comments about robot use, such as "Soon robots will replace teachers in classrooms" or "Robots will repair your drains so that you never need to call a plumber again." These far-fetched predictions will reflect badly on you and your employers, as readers will recall similar predictions made over the years that never came true. Unless, of course, you're talking about sex robots. We can all agree fully autonomous sex robots are gonna happen, if they haven't already.

- Pronouncing "robot" like "row-butt" is pretty funny.

"CONTROVERSIAL" TOPICS

Science often deals with big, seemingly open-ended questions, such as "How did the universe begin?" or "What are the origins of man?" or "Why does microwave popcorn always come out either burned or with dozens of unpopped kernels?"

Many people feel that such questions address the fundamental nature of man and his role in the universe and therefore are best answered by men of faith, not men of science. This often leads to controversy, as religious people feel belittled by scientific theories of man and the universe and rationalists feel that matters of belief have no place dictating, for example, school curricula or public policy.

Giving all sides an equal chance to share their views is very important. When it comes to the possibility that global warming is caused by human behavior, the opinion of a man with an MBA who does consulting work for oil companies is just as valid as the opinion of a man with multiple doctorates in climatology and chemistry and thirty years' experience studying the planet's climate. The opinions of the former may even be more useful, as he is less likely to be prejudiced by spending too much time on the subject.

It is best to tread lightly around these matters. Any hint of condescension in your coverage will lead, at best, to angry letters to your editors. The worst-case scenario would be a repeat of the Chicago "Devil's Kernels" riots of 1983. Methodists take their popcorn very seriously.

Global Warming

Global warming is a contentious topic, inspiring heated (ahem) debates, complaints, and outright anger whenever it is brought up, with people denying that it is happening even as the grain belt slowly moves upward into Canada. Therefore, you should write about global warming as often as possible to attract readership, viewers, advertising money, or whatever it is that keeps you afloat financially or mentally. When doing so, keep the following in mind:

- No matter what you write about climate-change science, your editor is going to put a picture of a sad polar bear on a tiny iceberg right next to your article, so don't be surprised when you see it.

- Any mentions of the irony of Al Gore inventing the Internet, leading to the widespread use of millions of energy-guzzling computers that only exacerbate global warming, will earn you a punch in the mouth, and rightfully so.

- Always mention any cold weather occurring at the same time as a conference on global warming. Even if it's winter. Even if it's not anywhere close to the conference. Even if global warming doesn't actually mean all cold weather everywhere has suddenly stopped.

- Include quotes from politicians and pundits who criticize environmentalists and celebrity activists for traveling to climate-change awareness events via jumbo jets and SUVs, but only if said politicians and pundits can prove that they only ride bicycles and take public transportation.

- We're not saying not to mention cow farts when talking about climate change, but, dude: cow farts. That's hysterical.

STORMS OF THE CENTURY

For some reason—either God's wrath or normal weather patterns—"storms of the century" are happening with more frequency than trials of the century. With that in mind, it's important to indicate the unprecedented size of the storm by coming up with a catchy portmanteau. Here are some suggestions:

Snowmaggedon
Snowicane
Snownami
Snowpedemic
Snowquake
Snowdenburg
Snowshtar
Snowdemonium
Snowpocalypse
Snowlocaust
Snowlcano
The Snowshank Redemption
Gensnowcide
Snowtanic
Snow! The Humanity!
The Jay Leno Snow

Evolution

Discussions of evolution should always emphasize that it is only a theory, much in the same way that "the theory of light" implies that light may not exist and "the theory of gravity" implies that what goes up could just as easily keep going up.

Challenges to the teaching of evolution, such as claims of "academic freedom" or "teaching the controversy" or "allowing for alternative viewpoints," may, for reasons of space, be collectively referred to as "a load of horseshit."

MATHEMATICS (SUKS LOL)

When writing about mathematics, keep in mind that, more than any other subject, it's the one your audience (a) hates and fears and (b) has been assured it is good and right to hate and fear. Thanks to twenty years of high-school-education programs that are designed to make people comfortable with not knowing math, and thanks to a prevalent social attitude that even simple addition is an arcane form of wizardry that normal people just aren't equipped to handle, the moment you mention any kind of numerical manipulation, most of your audience will behave as though you just started speaking in a previously unknown dialect of Martian.

The first thing you have to do is assure your readers that the math won't be too painful and that they can skip it if they want to. Of course, the reason you're even bringing up math in the first place is that it underpins whatever you're talking about, so don't be surprised when they bitch later about the fact that you "never bothered to explain any of it."

At the same time, don't try too hard to make the math portions of your writing understandable. If someone with a nontechnical background reads it and realizes they can actually follow what you're saying, the result will not be a lightbulb going off and the realization that maybe math isn't so scary. They will instead make sure no one saw them doing math and, if anyone was watching, they'll explain that, ha ha, they just happened to open up the newspaper to some math: Oh, man, what was THAT doing there? I must have picked up someone else's paper because, no sir, not me—math is gay.

SPECIAL NUMBERS

The world of numbers has had many breakthroughs in which previously unknown or unconsidered numbers were allowed into the fold. The strange nature of these later additions can be seen in their names.

negative numbers Numbers less than zero.
irrational numbers Values, such as pi, that can't be expressed as a ratio of two whole numbers.
imaginary numbers Values involving the square root of –1.
absurd numbers Values involving division by zero.
the youarefuckingkiddingme sequence Integers that lie between existing integers.
Thesenumbersareridiculousleavemyofficeatonce numbers Numbers you need special goggles to even see. Named for Dr. Anton Thesenumbersareridiculousleavemyofficeatonce at the University of Heidelburg.

GLOSSARY

absolute zero Man, remember Chasley X. Poindexter back in eighth grade? What a loser that guy was! Face fulla zits, always striking out with the girls, always smelled like corn chips?

alcohol What scientists drink while waiting for their grant money.

angstrom Unit for measuring existential fear.

aquifer An underground area containing water. When capitalized, the name of the demonic being that rules over these areas.

aromatic ring What Dr. Nilson keeps joking about whenever he farts, and frankly, the rest of the guys in the lab are sick of it.

black hole Collapsed star with a gravity field so enormous not even light can escape (e.g., Marlon Brando).

carcinogen Anything that can cause cancer. In short, everything.

classical physics Physics with lots of woodwind instruments and violins and shit, not like cool rock 'n' roll physics with guitar riffs and drum solos. You can keep your old people's physics, Grandpa!

closed system A physical system that does not allow the introduction of foreign elements; made illegal by desegregation laws in the 1960s.

continuous sample When you just can't stop pooping.

empirical law Laws established and used by the Empire until they were overthrown by Luke Skywalker and the Rebel Alliance.

Erdos number Descriptor of an individual's proximity to the prolific Hungarian mathematician Paul Erdos (analogous to Six Degrees of Kevin Bacon). If Erdos coauthored a paper with A, and B coauthored one with A, and C with B, and D with C, then D's Erdos number would be four. The Bureau Chiefs have an Erdos number of three. So suck it, Carl Sagan!

etymology The study of words. Not to be confused with "entomology," the study of sentient talking trees.

free radical Abbie Hoffman.

gaseous diffusion Wildly waving your hands around in the elevator after you let one rip and before anyone else gets on.

Halley's Comet Named for Sir Edmond Halley, this celestial body regularly appears in the sky every seventy-six years.

Haley's Comet Named for Haley Joel Osment, this celestial body irregularly appears in the sky every time a child actor with some modicum of talent shows up.

Heisenberg's uncertainty principle We think it's something to do with the fact that the more accurate a measurement you have of one element, the less accurate a measurement you have of another related element, but we're not entirely sure.

hypothesis A testable explanation for an observable phenomenon. It is not actually necessary for anyone to have tested a hypothesis before you report on the AMAZING NEW BREAKTHROUGH IN WEIGHT REDUCTION!!!

Jurassic period 199.6–145.5 million years ago, or October 24, 4004 BC, 12:17 p.m.–3:44 p.m. for creationists.

LASER An acronym meaning "light amplification by stimulated emission of radiation." Should always be printed in full caps; see: **SCUBA, SNAFU, GAYDAR.**

Maxwell's demon Thought experiment by physicist James Maxwell in which he posited a being that would look totally boss when airbrushed on the side of his van. Maxwell's demon inspired Kelvin's dragon, the emblem on Lord Kelvin's Trans Am.

parsec Unit of time for measuring how long it takes one to complete the Kessel Run.

periodic table The table you bring out when you've got guests.

Phenomena 1985 horror film directed by Dario Argento. Scientists are big horror fans.

radiation Particles and/or rays that emanate from the nuclei of atoms. Exposure will give you superpowers.

ratio That guy Hamlet's talking to in the graveyard.

Schrödinger's cat Always simultaneously capitalized and not capitalized.

standard deviation Like, you know, furry handcuffs or stuff like that, things vanilla folks use to make themselves think they're kinky.

subchronic Really awful weed that the skeezy guy over on Third Street sells. It's cheap, but you get what you pay for. Better off just waiting for Tall Jim to replenish his stock.

theory In science, the best explanation for an observable phenomenon given all the available evidence. In other words, a random guess.

Uranus Seventh planet from the sun. Yes, we know the name sounds like "your anus," but save the butthole jokes. You're a grown adult and a professional writer, for God's sake.

water table A novelty furniture piece that seemed amusing when you were in the store looking at it but, now that you've had it at home for a while, is kind of more trouble than it's worth.

<9>

PSEUDOSCIENCE AND THE SUPERNATURAL:

YA RLY

Ghosts. Flying saucers. Creationism. Homeopathy. The Loch Ness monster. Remote viewing. Psychics. Dowsing. Acupuncture. Bigfoot.

Yes, we all know it's bullshit, but boy howdy, do these things draw in the readers. Nearly all responsible journalists, even those at the *Washington Post*, are rightfully appalled at the space wasted on topics rife with logical fallacies and delusional beliefs. But as we've already covered politics in a previous chapter, let's stick to pseudoscience and the paranormal.

It certainly seems like a paradox that at this peak of technological and cultural advancement, with information shared the world over, humanity finds itself marching firmly backward in time. Far too large a percentage of the world's populace appears nostalgic for an era when diseases were caused by unbalanced humors and treated with leeches, when lights and sounds in the sky were caused by angry gods, when the local fortune-teller provided guidance, and that the weird, sorta logish shape in the lake was a horrible, red-toothed sea serpent.

Like it or not, this is your readership, a readership that wallows in its own ignorance of the world and—again paradoxically—turns to outlets that attempt to inform and educate, such as yours. However, should you try to correct your readers' misconceptions, if you dare to tell them that the government is not suppressing the water-powered car or that chupacabras aren't hunting bigfoots in their flying saucers, they're the ones who are going to leave nasty messages on your office voice mail or send you . . . things . . . in the mail.

But hey, in these trying times, you're grateful for anyone who's willing to pay for your publication when they can get the same info for free online. A customer's a customer, and if they want their biases confirmed, you're the man and/or woman for the job!

THE BASICS

When covering potentially controversial scientific claims, it is necessary to treat all claims with skepticism in order to maintain the appearance of journalistic impartiality. Scientists don't *know* that climate change has a human origin, after all.

The same is true when it comes to reporting on supernatural claims, only in reverse. In order to maintain an impartial tone, you must report all stories of supernatural goings-on with complete credulity. These aren't easily explainable phenomena; they're mysteries . . . *FOR THE AGES.*

Here are mistakes to avoid when covering some of these topics.

Reparative Therapy

Many people hold that being gay or lesbian is a choice, but one that can only be undone with divine intervention.

However, under no circumstances should you ask these people if prayer can also change your eye color or remove that vaguely satanic widow's peak from your hairline.

Intelligent Design

When offered a banana as proof that there is a designer, refrain from pointing out that the fruit commonly sold in grocery stores is actually a seedless, cultivated descendant of the wild banana.

Under no circumstances mention dog breeding or the flu when it is argued that it is impossible to observe evolution in action.

Fairies

Do not make fun of the spelling. Whatever spelling they use.

Considered to be truly ridiculous even by people who chronicle the movements of Bat Boy across the Gulf Coast, most of the people who believe in fairies are girls with faulty bullshit detectors and vast collections of corsets. Play your cards right and you'll get two stories: one for your publication and one about a wild time behind the funnel-cake tent at the ren fair.

Mediums

Do not fuck with the cold reading and answer "yes" to every question.

Although definitive proof of the persistence of human consciousness (or "soul") past death has profound implications for every religious and philosophical system known to man, refrain from asking the medium why the departed limit their communications with the living to toothless platitudes rather than serious theological discussions. The living are probably better off not knowing that the dead are condemned to spend eternity writing motivational posters.

Hauntings

Do not point out that the ghost detector is just a stud finder painted green.

Do not make "whoo whoo" noises behind the backs of the ghost hunters.

Do not adjust the thermostat to make the haunted rooms colder.

UFOs

Do not ever, under any circumstances, point out that the photo of the alien craft is clearly just a plate held aloft on a thin string.

Avoid pointing out that faster-than-light-speed travel is a physical impossibility.

Don't ask why the only people who ever seem to encounter aliens are drunken hillbillies. It's not clever or original when racist ventriloquists make it part of their act. Just let it go.

BIGFOOT SIGHTINGS

Bigfoot reports come in very few varieties and may be divided up as follows:

- "We saw a big, hairy man in the woods!" (Probably Hobo Jim lettin' it all hang out on a warm afternoon. Don't get too excited.)
- "We have photographic proof of bigfoot!" (Almost certainly the same blurry photograph of something brownish you always see, despite camera technology improving by leaps and bounds in both portability and photo quality over the last decade or two.)
- "Bigfoot climbed inside his flying saucer and vanished into the fifteenth dimension, right before my eyes!" (Even by bigfoot-story standards, this is just plain bug-fuck crazy. Avoid at all costs.)
- "I shot bigfoot, and I'm going to display its body!" (If it's not just a fake made with a cheap bigfoot costume, then pray it's not poor old Hobo Jim.)

ON INTERVIEWING PSYCHICS

The problem with doing features on psychics is that they tend to be squirrelly people, slippery and evasive, and the ones that aren't outright frauds are instead in need of medication. As such, they'll do anything to avoid giving you an answer that's either clear-cut or easily verifiable.

Psychics are big attention grabbers, though, so suck it up and do your best to work with them. Maybe you can wring out a story that'll satisfy your editors, please your readers, bring in ad revenue, and, let's hope, keep you out of a courtroom.

- If the psychics regularly make predictions, either of the "Here's what I see for the coming year" kind or simply tossed out as a matter of course, do not pin them down on their accuracy rates. Throwing the truth—that their hit rate is about on par with that of your average *Star Wars* storm trooper—in their faces will only serve to piss them off, and there goes your story.

- If a psychic claims to have assisted in police investigations by providing exact details of, say, where to find the body of a murder victim, it's bad form to ask why the police didn't arrest the psychic as a possible suspect.

- When you ask psychics about the cash prizes some organizations offer to people who can prove paranormal abilities under scientific observation, they're going to give you excuses like "Oh, they won't give up that money" or "I can't call up my powers on demand," which you should dutifully and sympathetically record. Do not shout "Chicken!" at them and make clucking noises, no matter how good that would feel. Oh, man. So good.

- We know it's tempting to say, "Guess what I'm going to ask next!" but that's really not recommended. It's funny, sure, but don't do it.

- If you plan on asking the psychic how he or she feels about the fraudulent psychics cluttering the field, you may want to practice the question at home a few times to make sure you can get through it without bursting out in laughter.

- Psychics will answer your questions with vague talk about spirits and angels and energy and flashes of insight and intuition and stuff floating around in the air around us. None of it will make any damned sense, but just transcribe it and throw it in the article. People will eat it up.

- If a psychic brings up the fact that there are still things science can't explain, do your best to keep from reminding him or her that most scientists are not legally obligated to say that their findings are for entertainment purposes only.

- Asking how much the psychic makes via readings, personal sittings, phone consultations, and so on may catch him or her out for being shifty, since the psychic will be reluctant to reveal his or her high profits for fear of negative publicity. On the other hand, if you find out how much psychics make, you'll probably quit your low-paying writing job and start performing readings yourself.

UFO REPORTS

There's more interest in possible alien visitations than ever, as science fiction has trained gullible viewers everywhere to look to the skies in the hope that someone will come to take them away to a computer-generated world of gigantic blue cat-Smurfs. If your editor is, you know, a bit teched, or just has a perverse sense of humor, you may find yourself on the UFO beat, talking to wide-eyed true believers about the flashing light in the sky they just happened to see, um, over the airport or by the fireworks show. Here are a few questions you'll need to ask your sources to fill those column inches:

- How big was the UFO?
- How fast was it moving?
- How far away was it?
- Are you particularly skilled at determining exact sizes, speeds, and distances of faraway, fast-moving, indistinct objects?
- Was the full moon out?
- Was the object you saw actually the full moon?
- Was it perhaps someone mooning you?
- How much have you been drinking?
- What were you drinking?
- Oh, yeah, that's some good sauce. What'd you pay?

- So, did anyone else see this object?
- I mean besides your cat?
- Or your other cat.
- Just out of curiosity . . . do you have a history of bigfoot sightings?
- Are you sure it wasn't a plane?
- Or maybe a streetlamp?
- Maybe you were near a "rave," with the kids and their big hats and their "glow sticks." No? You sure?
- Did the object land?
- Did any beings disembark from the craft?
- Were they wearing blue uniforms with badges, and did they make you attempt to walk in a straight line?
- In this photo of yours, is this string attached to the top of the craft that looks like a pie tin perhaps a tether to its mother ship?
- How many seasons of *The X-Files* do you have on DVD?
- That many, huh?

GLOSSARY

alternative medicine Medicine that came to prominence in the nineties, originating in Seattle after the peak of grunge medicine's popularity.

ancient astronauts Theory that alien visitors were responsible for amazing feats of engineering and knowledge otherwise attributed to some ancient nonwhite race.

Area 51 Military base in Nevada near that ████████ ████████ and the ████████ for ████████ around ████████ since ████████.

astrology The scientific study of George Jetson's dog.

Atlantis Legendary ancient civilization credited with astonishing scientific, cultural, and spiritual accomplishments. It seems that these developments did not include the invention of the boat, as some unknown catastrophe is thought to have destroyed the island nation.

Bermuda Triangle Popular method of sculpting one's pubic hair.

Big Pharma Derogatory term for drug companies that are hiding cures for all major diseases because then they'd be out of business, maaaaan. While all arguments using this term may be safely disregarded, they must still be included in stories for "balance."

Breatharianism The belief in the body's ability to survive simply by breathing air and by secretly eating food when no one is looking.

Breatharyanism The belief in the body's ability to survive simply by breathing the purified air of the Master Race.

channelling See: **pretending.**

chupacabra Cheap Mexican knockoff monster that has taken monstering jobs away from hardworking American monsters.

Clever Hans phenomenon Occurrence in which a thief (though usually an exceptional one) will, under certain circumstances, appear as an international terrorist. First manifested around Christmas of 1988, in Nakatomi Plaza, Los Angeles.

cold reading Game of "twenty questions" with enormous cash payouts.

Creationism The belief that life did not evolve over time but was, in fact, created as is by an all-powerful being. Contradicted by every bit of science ever, thanks to a pact between scientists and Satan.

crop circles A phenomenon completely unexplainable to people who have heard the terms "FTL drive," "Alpha Centauri," and "Whitley Streiber," but not "boards," "strapped," "to," or "feet."

cryptozoologist Adobe Photoshop expert.

demonic possession Nine tenths of demonic law.

electronic voice phenomenon Science-y sounding term that roughly translates as "broken radio" or "defective recorder" or "hearing things that aren't there."

fairy Two little girls fooled Sherlock Holmes creator Sir Arthur Conan Doyle with faked photographs of these mythical creatures, which just goes to show you.

Geller, Uri Alleged psychic who bends spoons with his mind, despite the fact that it's quicker and easier to bend them with one's hands and despite the fact that nobody needs bent spoons.

haint A colloquial term for "ghost" from the southern United States. Much funnier sounding than "ghost" and should be used whenever possible, preferably in the format of "Oh Lordy, it's a haint!"

homeopathic theory .

hundredth-monkey phenomenon Phenomenon that, frankly, could use even more monkeys.

indigo children Children who have been told they are magical space geniuses who will forever change society and for some reason are insufferably spoiled.

intelligent design Should be used in place of "creationism" only when the maximum ironic potential of the term "intelligent" is reached.

lake creatures A mysterious form of aquatic life fond of establishing profitable relationships with struggling tourist traps.

medium Person who claims to be able to communicate with spirits. Ironically, most are at LEAST a large.

MKULTRA Top secret CIA program designed to beat the Soviets' top score on Mortal Kombat.

moon-landing hoax Conspiracy theory claiming the same government that used alien technology to kill JFK with Atlantean psychic bullets had to fake the moon landing.

orbs Restless spirits who have shed their mortal bodies and taken on the mystical forms of out-of-focus dust motes.

Ouija board Device in which a flat pointer is moved around to reveal messages from elsewhere. See: **e-mail.**

perpetual-motion machine Concept that expresses a base sort of irony in that the only thing perpetual about this kind of machine is that people keep thinking they've invented one.

precognition The ability to make statements so vague that people believe a sixteenth-century French poet wrote them.

psychic Should not be placed in quotes, even though it really should always be placed in quotes.

psychic surgery Method by which, without benefit of medical instruments or anesthesia, money is extracted from a patient's bank account.

quantum mechanics Whatever you want it to mean, sport!

remote viewing The ability to find lost remote controls behind seat cushions or under the coffee table from great distances away.

science The discipline responsible for, among other things, cars, television, and the Internet.

SCIENCE! The discipline responsible for, among other things, Frankenstein's monster, mind-control helmets, and orbital death lasers.

sheep-and-goats phenomenon Explanation for why psychic powers seem to be dampened when skeptics are present and cheating is guarded against. This is the reason why ice placed in a hot skillet will not melt if enough people present believe it won't.

skunk ape See: **your mom.**

sleep paralysis Also known as "old hag syndrome," this well-documented and well-understood phenomenon nevertheless baffles at least one *Fortean Times* letter writer a month.

telekinesis Psychic ability that, due to advances in

skepticism and cheat preventing, has gone from being able to make tables rise and move about to being able to slightly alter microstresses in materials.

Tesla Pioneer of radio, discoverer of alternating current, and inventor of the magnetic etheric psychic death ray. Also a heavy-metal band currently rockin' the state fair circuit.

<10>

WEAPONS AND THE MILITARY:

SHOOT FIRST, THEN ASK QUESTIONS ABOUT SHOOTING

War! Huh! Good God, y'all! What is it good for? A sharp increase in circulation!

Warfare is the second-most-powerful engine of economic and technological advancement, after porn. A brief attempt to combine the two during World War II saw one unit sent to liberate Paris clad in crotchless hot pink latex chaps, and while the Geneva Convention eventually banned this practice as "criminal weirding out," the operation was a technical success and a key factor in the Allied defeat of the Third Reich. And more important, pictures from the front line (and an average of six inches in front of the front line) set sales records for the *San Francisco Chronicle* that have yet to be beaten.

You'd think living under the constant threat of nuclear apocalypse for most of the twentieth century would've dulled the public's enthusiasm for stories about bombs, explosions, and other forms of armed combat, but believe us: Readers just can't get enough of it. It's your job to bring the excitement of the front line to the front page, and since our legal department has informed us that actually shooting at your readers while they do the Jumble is a catastrophically bad idea, you're going to have to do it with your words. Sure, filling your column inches with lurid statistics about how many people could be killed with the ordnance on your average aircraft carrier might seem like an exploitative, crass tactic that minimizes the actual sacrifice soldiers make every day, but just consider this: Michael Bay is a millionaire.

THE BASICS

As mandated by the Top Gun Act of 1984, every soldier you interview should have a **colorful nickname** related to both his personality and his military training. If for some reason you're interviewing a soldier who doesn't have a nickname, you may invent one. It's probably best to stick to names like "Ace" and "Sergeant Badass" rather than "Sweatballs" and "Pretty Princess," as those guys have combat training and remote-control bombing drones at their disposal.

#

When writing about weapons, a reporter is encouraged to use shortened or generic terms (for example, "AK-47" and "rifle") on second reference but should initially provide all available information using the following conventions:

- Magical attack bonuses should **precede** the name of the item and are always written as numerals. *The +5 long sword had largely fallen out of favor by the end of the Vietnam War.*

- Other mystical qualities should be listed **after** the item. *While not technically a weapon, the Dildo of Endless Penetration is considered a key element in a dozen armed robberies in the greater Rohan area.*

- Trademarked weaponry should be named **along with** its maker. *Could a local vigilante's exclusive use of the Wayne Industries Batarang™ be a sign of insider trading?*

Being sent off to serve as target practice for insurgents in a 140-degree desert might seem like a harsh punishment for what you did at the last press club Christmas party, but keep in mind that war correspondents have a proud and noble history. Do your job right and your name will go down in history alongside Civil War photographer Mathew Brady, whose memory is kept alive every year at countless Civil War photography reenactments; Martin Degrell, who tragically lost his life covering the cola wars; and of course Hector Ramirez, whose coverage of our twenty-year conflict with Cobra gave America's daring, highly trained Special Forces unit the information they needed to defeat the Weather Dominator.

#

"World War" should only be used for conflicts involving countries on at least three continents. For large-scale battles against clones, killer tomatoes, or a fifty-foot woman, use "attack" instead.

#

When writing about **military personnel**, it is imperative that you get their ranks correct. Lucky for you, the ranks in every military branch are exactly the same as those on *Star Trek*:

- cadet
- ensign
- red shirt
- doctor
- chief petty officer (only applicable to personnel who run transporters)

- lieutenant junior grade
- lieutenant
- whatever Data was

FREQUENTLY CONFUSED WORDS

bore/boor The bore is the interior of a firearm's barrel, not counting the chamber. A boor is the exterior of someone who gives a crap, not counting police and military personnel.

caliber/calibre The diameter of a gun barrel; the diametre of a gun barrle.

canon/cannon Canon is what is considered an official part of a work, such as the Bible or *Star Wars*. A cannon is what you want to shoot at people who won't shut the fuck up about canon.

fissile/fizzle *The missile with the fissile material fizzled, which caused us to whistle rather than pissle.*

ordnance/ordinance *There is an ordinance against deploying ordnance within the city limits. Thanks a lot, B. Hussein Obama.*

right/excuse Generally an American foible. See: the Second Amendment.

semiautomatic/automatic A semiautomatic firearm fires one cartridge, ejects the used case, and reloads the chamber with each trigger pull. An automatic is for the people.

side car/sidecar Conveyance attached to a motorcycle; cocktail attached to Mumsy's left hand after five o'clock.

Winchester/Worcestershire These are never confused, but now you'll be saying "Winchester, Worcestershire" all day. You're welcome.

- commander
- science officer
- captain
- admiral
- Q

#

Phonetically spell out the sounds of war for maximum reporting impact. Common battlefield sounds:

Heavy machine gun: HUBBA DUBBA DUBBA

Assault rifle: Geddy Lee! Geddy-Geddy Lee!

Uzi: Cha! Cha-cha-cha!

Mortar explosion: THOOOM!

Distant mortar explosion: . . . ThoooM . . .

TIPS FOR EMBEDDED REPORTERS

So you've pissed off your boss and are now being sent to Afghanistan, where you'll be embedded with a unit of tough Army Rangers. Don't panic. You're more likely to get killed driving to work in the morning than you are in a lawless war zone like Afghanistan.

Actually, that's total bullshit—you're WAY more likely to

die in Afghanistan. We were just hoping you'd stop reading after "Don't panic."

Increase your chances of survival by following these fun and easy tips:

Cultivate a crazy James Woods state of mind: The manic, intense actor James Woods is an excellent behavioral role model for embedded reporters. We don't know why, but it just works. We recommend repeatedly viewing his films *Salvador* and *The Hard Way* and developing a fiendish cocaine habit before your assignment for a properly edgy mental state.

Practice your haunted stare: Spend some time perfecting your "thousand-yard stare" so that you can adopt the weary glamour of a journalist who has been in The Shit. This comes in handy at boring staff meetings and at dinner parties.

Get a fishing vest: Trust us, you will totally fit in if you wear a fishing vest. Not recommended: neon hunting jackets.

Strive to maintain your journalistic objectivity: At no point in your time with the troops should you let them know whom you want to win the war.

Learn about Afghanistan (optional): You might want to learn a little bit about Afghanistan before you leave. If pressed for time, just watch *Rambo III* on the flight over—he plays goat polo with Mujahideen in that one. It's awesome.

OR . . .

Do you really want to risk tripping a Bouncing Betty for an article that's just going to be upstaged by a report about a high-school fashion show? Now that cell phones and Wi-Fi have made it possible to file stories from almost anywhere in the world, why travel at all? Snuggle in under the covers and tell your editor you're "embedded."

KNOW YOUR BOMBS

Given mankind's knack for creating newer and better ways to destroy things, it can be difficult to keep track of them all. Here's a quick reference guide to the more commonly encountered infernal devices.

atomic bomb Uses the power of nuclear fission to enormous destructive effect.

anatomic bomb Uses the power of killer abs to stunningly sexy effect.

neutron bomb Kills people, leaves buildings intact. Priorities, you know.

hydrogen bomb An atomic bomb that has been super-sized with tritium and a side order of chicken fries.

mother of all bombs Precision munition designed to lie awake at night wondering why you didn't call in from the target zone and whether you were lying, undetonated in a crater somewhere.

smart bomb A munition that has won the General Dynamics book award along with a $250 scholarship.

stupid bomb *Gigli.*

really stupid bomb Will Smith's remake of *Wild Wild West.*

da bomb A weapon of mass awesomeness (e.g., last week's Bureau Chiefs' kegger, the latest Gorillaz remix, the time we javelin-spammed that noob in *Modern Warfare 2*).

IED Birth control device that works by . . . Wait, this cannot be right.

nude bomb A tragic weaponization of a beloved sixties sitcom.

F-bomb Prone to backfire disastrously if deployed in front of your mom or your Sunday school teacher.

sex bomb Tom Jones. (The **mother of all bombs** is a huge fan.)

conventional bomb Owns a ranch silo in the suburbs, has 2.3 bomblets, listens to Dave Matthews.

dirty bomb What most conventional bombs daydream about being.

***Dirrty* bomb** Device used to destroy the last vestiges of Christina Aguilera's teenybopper image.

Cherry Bomb A runaway device designed to be deployed by a Jett or a Ford.

Ch-ch-ch-cherry Bomb The above device, fully primed and armed.

pipe bomb Should not be mistaken for a "pipe bong."

FOREIGN WARS

This may come as a massive shock, but not all wars involve the United States, at least not directly. Foreign wars are like foreign cuisine, offering a sanitized taste of exotic lands that makes readers appreciate their mayo on white bread all the more.

Before conducting an interview with a **child soldier**, be sure to get permission from his or her parents and/or coke-addicted warlord first.

Do not use "tsk-tsk" in stories about brutal third-world insurgencies. That's already implied.

Each time an **African regime changes**, it's its own

specific case, and you should take extra care when you do a find-and-replace on dictators' names.

Jokes about the French retreating at the first sign of resistance are always good for a laugh, provided you and your audience know nothing about history.

Do not suggest that **land mines** provide a great way to lose weight.

GLOSSARY

AK-47 One of several bounty hunters hired by Darth Vader to capture Han Solo.

BFG A large, highly destructive weapon perfect for killing demons; named for its developers, Bigg, Focking, and Gunn.

Black Hawk A military helicopter, a hockey team, a comic-book island base of operations, or a hawk that is black. Don't confuse them.

broadsword Bladed weapon used by dames, hey-OHHH!

Dalek A mobile battle tank composed of dalekanium and piloted by a Skaro mutant. Not a fucking robot.

Death Star II Renamed "Wilhuff Tarkin Memorial Hope Star" in an effort to achieve bipartisan support.

embedded Fuckin'.

evasive maneuvers "The, uh, perfume-counter lady spritzed me is all. That's why I smell that way."

Excalibur A sword some guy got from some drowning lady or maybe found in a rock and that made him king somehow. See: **Electoral College.**

Excalibur caliber The ammunition measurement of a gun that shoots swords that make people kings.

freedom fighter A white insurgent.

Glamdring The sword that finally brought English rocker Gary Glitter to justice.

gun See: **gat, heater, six-shooter, piece, mac, nine, strap, phallic symbol, Hemingway's last meal.**

lightsaber A cavalry sword made from aluminum rather than heavy steel.

megaton An explosive force equivalent to one million tons of TNT. Do not confuse with male porn star Megatongue.

M-16 Before writing about the M-16, get your readers up to speed with a brief synopsis of *M*s 1–15.

NORAD Not radical.

Predator drone When the Predator will just not shut the fuck up about all the skulls he's collected.

radar Special sense allowing men named Ray to detect other men named Ray.

rail gun A giant gun that shoots trains instead of bullets. That's how fucking giant it is.

seaman Go ahead, giggle. . . . Get it out of your system.

sniper Tom Berenger's finest performance.

sonar Text-message abbreviation for "So not all right." *OMG Becky, I drank 23 PBRs last night and then Brad wouldn't even hold my hair. That's SONAR.*

trebuchet It's all like, CREAAAAAK and then WOOOOOOOOSH and then CRAAAAAAAAAASH, and the other dudes are all, NOOOOOOOO.

vorpal blade Beware: although all vorpal blades go snicker-snack, not all blades that go snicker-snack are vorpal.

WMDs Aaaaaany day now.

<11>

CITATION AND ATTRIBUTION:

DO NOT HIT THE SNOOZE BUTTON

BUY SOCKS

Let's face it:

When it comes to citing sources,

you are fucked.

There are 356 different citation formats, thirty-two of which require you to know the author's blood type in order to complete your citation. Citation formats include MLA, APA, CMS, CSE, CSS, CBGBs, CREAM, ASS, JLA, SARS, MGMT, TCB, and Batman, just to name a few. To be an effective writer in this day and age, you have to know all of them. Or you can just make shit up and rely on the fact that no one else knows this stuff either. Take your best shot.

The rapid evolution of media over the past few years has outpaced even the most conscientious editors, so that by the time they finally settle on a way to properly cite You-Tube comments (username, date, the episode of *Fraggle Rock* the video came from, and the number of racial slurs left in the comments), Twitter comes along and the cycle starts all over again.

That (along with the rush of power and profitability that comes from forcing an entire industry to obey an arbitrary set of rules you made up) is why we've decided to come up with our own citation format. We will give you the tools you need to cover the things that really matter while those other nerds continue to snobbishly ignore new media in favor of reminders that telegraph wires can't transmit italics.

Seriously. *Telegraph wires.*

HOW TO CITE . . .

ONLINE SOURCES

Author. "Title of article." Type of article. Name of website. Retrieved from <<URL of website>>. Explanation of URL. Medium of delivery. Explanation of Internet. [[Time and date resource was retrieved (in GMT)]]. {{Browser type. ^Operating System^}}. *supplementary information.*

> Sims, Christopher J., Esq. "I Love Corn Dogs Almost More Than Face Kicking." Comment left on author's blog. Chris's Invincible Super-Blog. Retrieved from <http://www.the-isb.com/?p=2432#comments>>. A URL is a Uniform Resource Locator, a computing term popularized in the mid-1990s by Tim Berners-Lee, who now regrets the use of backslashes. While the Internet was originally created as part of the government agency ARPA, it has now evolved into the popular communications medium where people can post videos of cats playing pianos. The first Web browser, Mosaic, was developed in Urbana, Illinois. So was the computer Hal in *2001*. I'm just pointing out an interesting coincidence. I'm not saying that the Internet will develop artificial human intelligence and rise up to kill us all. [[Retrieved on 23:47 on October 28, 2009]]. {{Firefox. ^Mac OS X Version 10.5.8^}}. *October's Latin root means eight.*

Trendy Chinese Tattoos

Odds are a trendy Chinese character tattoo does not mean what the tattoo recipient thought it did. For these, cite the intended meaning, followed by the real meaning in brackets. Also include the location of the tattoo. "Lower back" may be replaced with "tramp stamp."

> Jones, Matt. "Strength [Supermarket]." Right bicep.

Graffiti

> Anon. "Here I Sit, Broken-Hearted, Tried to Shit, But Only Farted." Stall Three, Men's Room, Belvedere Oasis, Interstate 90, Rockford, IL. 30 March 2010.

Penthouse Forum Letters

Cite like any other work of fiction. You don't think stuff like this really happens, do you?

> Anon. "I never thought these stories were true until I pulled into that small-town gas station one stormy night." *Penthouse Forum*, June 1986.

Candid Interviews

> Woman in the doctor's waiting room who wouldn't shut up about her life. Nobody Wants to Know About Your Lower Intestine. Pp. 138–293.

Scholarly Works

Not exactly sure what this is. If you can't get it on the Internet, don't worry about it.

Hipster T-shirts

Include the owner of the shirt, the ironic slogan, and the year the slogan stopped being clever.

> McManus, Ray. "Virginia Is for Lovers." 2005.

Bumper Stickers

Include a description of the vehicle along with the location and date of the sighting. Feel free to pass judgment on the owner.

> Some dick in a Lexus. "When Guns Are Outlawed, Only Outlaws Will Have Guns." Mile marker 153, Interstate 95, Virginia. 12 December 2003.

Vanity Plates

Follows same rules as bumper sticker. You do not need to translate the vanity plate.

> Black Jetta. "I82NA." ShopRite Parking Lot, Magee Ave., Elizabeth, New Jersey. 17 January 2005.

Text Messages from Friends

Contrary to popular belief, text messages from your friends do need to be cited, and they may be used as supporting evidence and expert opinion in your research.

Carly. "OMG Devin SUX LOL!" 22 October 2010.

Your Crazy Neighbor's Dale Earnhardt Memorial Yard Display

Johnson, Jeff and Molly. "3 the Intimidator: Never Forgotten." Seriously, You Should See This Thing. It Takes Up the Whole Freaking Yard! It's Got Bright Red Lights and Sound Effects, and They Never Shut the Damn Thing Off! 642 Saint Christopher Drive, Florence, South Carolina.

Deez Nuts

Right here.

Your Uncle's Inappropriate Jokes

Be sure to cite only the setup and not the punch line, so as not to ruin the joke for your readers.

Uncle Al. "What Did the Leper Say to the Prostitute?" Thanksgiving dinner, 1989.

Your Mother's Advice

Siegel, Esther. "Don't mind me. No, really. You don't need to cite me at all. I give you advice all your life, but do you take it? No. Look at your cousin Noah; he's a successful doctor. I bet my sister doesn't cry herself to sleep at night from worrying about her child." When Will You Get Married and Give Me Grandchildren Already? Pp. 56–1009.

Your Own Sense of Crushing Despair and Ennui

Sheadsel, Joe. "Why did I decide to major in English?" Will I Work at a Coffee Shop with No Health Insurance for the Rest of My Life? Pp. 45–47.

Your Failed Relationship

Amber, Tiffanyee, and Jenni Clavicle. "Never Date a Drummer: A Play in Three Acts." Rue, Sorrow, and Remorse Theatrical Press. Climax, Michigan. 1997.

Annoying Facebook and Twitter Apps

Everest, Ludmilla. "A wandering purple cow is in my field. Please feed it some rutabaga. Poke! Also, weed my garden. Poke poke! In addition, click here to help me assassinate a mafia boss. Poke!" Foursquare Foursquare Foursquare Foursquare Foursquare Foursquare

Foursquare Foursquare and Foursquare Foursquare. Turn Off Your Computer and/or Phone and Take a Walk Already Press. 2011.

Reactions to New Apple Product Announcements

Jaah, Schlomindy. "I don't know. I've read the Apple rumor blogs and I think it will be lame. . . . Wait? It does what?! And it is as thin as five horizontally stacked mouse whiskers?! Is there a waitlist?!" Sorry I Don't Have an Extra $3,000 Right Now: A Quarterly Chapbook. January 27, 2010.

Street Crazies

Tall guy with the dog. Cardboard sign he was holding. Corner of Fifth and Thirty-fourth, New York, New York. About 3:15 p.m.

CITING PRINT SOURCES

If you are forced to cite a traditional print source, always abbreviate it as much as possible. This will make your data seem both mysterious and alluring. See if you can guess who these are!

U.S. Br. Lbr. Stat.	Pple. Mg.
Wll. St. Jrnl.	Pplr. Mchncs.
Wkly. Wrld. Nws.	Hstlr.
Glbl. Econ. Pros. & Devl. Cntr.	Wrd.

FOOTNOTES

Never use numbers when marking footnotes. Instead, use wingdings that complement the subject of your articles. For instance:

"*Jem and the Holograms*[❀] ably served as the prototype for third-wave animated[✏] feminism. Jerrica Benton exemplifies the female struggle toward self-actualization as she vainly attempts to find relevance in the male-dominated music industry. Only her id[⊙], in the form of the feminized computer and mother substitute Synergy, can aid Jerrica. It is significant that Synergy is an inheritance from Jerrica's dead father. As he constructs an artificial-intelligence replacement mother for the daughter, the daughter constructs her own new identity in the form of the rock star Jem[♉], providing a way for Jerrica to work through her unaddressed paternal issues."

❀ "Holograms and Unreality, My Psychotropia." Benton, Kimber. *Jem and the Holograms: My Life in Illusions*, pp. 23–45.

✏ "Why Did I Get Stuck with the Purple Hair?" Interview with Rio Pacheco, *People*, August 13, 1987.

⊙ Id, *The Freud Encyclopedia*, p. 4.

♉ *Pizzazz*. "Jem Is Not a Rock Star. I Am the Real Rock Star." Testimony before the Twelfth Subcommittee on Violence in Music. April 19, 1988.

PROPER ATTRIBUTION

In less formal writing, like for a magazine or a newspaper, you'll be asked to attribute quotes in your story to a source but not officially cite them. Be prepared to negotiate with your sources as to just what sort of conversation you'll be having, once you convince them that you're running the story about their illicit affair with a walrus whether they like it or not. These conversations typically fall into one of six categories:

"On the Record"

Unless the source tells you otherwise and you don't "accidentally" mishear or forget it, all your interviews will be in this category by default. A conversation being on the record means that you may use anything the source says, describe any of his or her mannerisms, and make fun of his or her weight, facial tics, and accent with abandon.

"Not for Attribution"

This means that the source prefers not to be named but that you may still use his or her quotes (or what you heard as the quotes) in your story. Rather than a name, however, you must identify the source with a description that the two of you agree on. For instance, if the vice president gives you information that's not for attribution, you may agree to refer to him as "someone who's almost president but isn't."

"On Background"

You must place the source's quotes behind the text of the rest of your story.

"Deep Background"

You may use the quotes, but they must be mixed into the fiber of the paper you print your story on. If it's a Web story, they must be hidden in the source code.

"Lobby Terms"

In the United Kingdom, journalists may be allowed to enter the restricted Members' Lobby in Westminster upon the conditions that what is said there never sees print and that they never leave.

"Off the Record"

Any information given off the record is intended to help you understand an issue but may never, ever, ever, ever, ever, ever, ever actually go into your story. It may be really juicy and make a great story, but you have to step off. It's supersecret. You should probably not even write it in your notes. In fact, forget we even said any of this. Forget this ever happened.

We're done here.

GLOSSARY

abstract What people do to make something look more deep than it is. If you want to do this in your writing, write with multicolored chalk and then smear it so your paragraphs look like expressionist paintings.

anonymous source Steve Johnson of 42 Rosebud Lane, Bainbridge Island, Washington (formerly Sal "The Knife" Botticelli of 3 West 22nd Street, Hoboken, New Jersey).

attribution See: **the rest of the chapter.**

Author Dudley Moore vehicle about the dangers of alcoholism.

bibliography See: **works cited list.**

editor Alcoholic.

endnote A note in your work proclaiming that the end is nigh.

fair use Anything available on the Internet is yours to use for free in any way you like. If it weren't free, why would it be on the Internet? See: **Creative Commons licenses.**

footnote A reminder written on your foot, like "Buy socks, stupid."

ibid A delicate deerlike creature that likes to nibble on leaves.

misquote A quote that gets all jammed up in the chamber.

paraphrase A superpower that renders its user intangible: *Kitty Pryde paraphrased through the wall to escape Juggernaut.*

parenthetical citation A citation that is also a hilarious aside.

peer review What the mean girls did when they said you were a loser for not having neon pink shoelaces.

primary source A source that is red, yellow, or blue.

quote What someone says. Or, you know, the general gist of it.

secondary source The other guy your main guy knows who might be able to score you something.

style guide The sales clerk at Nordstrom who helped you pick out a tie that harmonizes with your shirt.

supple A gymnast's limbs.

trans Use gender-neutral pronouns only when citing trans. Approved gender-neutral pronouns are "'e," "zhe," "they," and "thon."

trial balloon A balloon officials sometimes release with an idea attached. If someone finds the idea and sends it back, they'll know it's OK to raise taxes or buy a new stadium.

vol A small rodent. Beware of their burrowing ways.

works cited list See: **bibliography.**

<12>

PUNCTUATION AND GRAMMAR: LOL

WILL END
SENTENCES
FOR FOOD

English has undergone rapid changes in its history, much like the hyperevolution found on the planet Genesis in *Star Trek III: The Search for Spock.*

As the evolution of life on the planet accelerated after the triggering of the Genesis device, so have the rules of grammar and punctuation been buffeted by technological forces like text messaging, l33t speak, and the steady replacement of journalists by terrifying robots.

Truly, we live in a frightening time, when the ancient skill of diagramming a sentence may fade into obscurity as the human race evolves teeny tiny fingers attached to their main fingers in order to better mash cell-phone buttons.

Will grammar and punctuation remain constant in this strange new world? Likely not, but we will take a stand and codify the best punctuation and grammar rules in order to preserve English as we know it in a slab of amber, so that future generations will know to use quotation marks rather than italics.

(Meanwhile, by the time you buy this book, we'll probably have made fifteen arbitrary changes that can *and will* get you fired if you fail to use them. So basically, you can pretty much go nuts and ignore everything you're about to read. In fact, why not just rip these pages out of the book and burn them? Nothing means anything any longer. Oh God.)

THE BASICS

You are a wordsmith, and your art is a complex one that requires patience, study, and the correct ingredients.

Start with some high-quality wrought iron. The best writers also have several chisels and hammers. If you don't have your own anvil, your local university's English department might have some available for rent, since nobody majors in English anymore. Building a forge in your backyard takes a certain level of commitment, but do you want to be a better writer or not?

Your words must be heated to at least five hundred degrees before you strike them firmly with a hammer, forming them into a coherent sentence. Good writers must have phenomenal upper-body strength; John Updike had nineteen-inch biceps (unflexed), and James Frey's arms have been used in the "after" picture in a Charles Atlas advertisement.

Now grab that raw piece of wrought-iron news with your editing tongs and dip them where? In water? Oh, no, my friend. In a cooling liquid bath we like to call punctuation and grammar.

Continue to shape your paragraph on your anvil. When finished, apply a nice finish to your prose using a wire brush. Bluing is optional but can be used to excess. (Just look at Cormac "Ol' Blue Hands" McCarthy.) Nail your prose to the outside of your house to ward off fairies, or carefully pack it in a box of straw to send to your agent.

#

Think of **proper punctuation** as the thin blue line that separates the news from anarchy. A misplaced comma or an indirect clause could send an innocent man to prison. Desperate, he breaks out, a fugitive on the run in search of the reporter whose poor sentence construction landed him on death row. Suddenly, he shows up in the newsroom! You're at gunpoint! Why? Because of one botched semicolon. You son of a bitch. You *son of a bitch.*

#

An **adjective** modifies a noun. An **adverb** modifies a verb:

> His older lazy barking trombone salesman brother walked very sullenly down the hallway.

Avoid using **absolute modifiers** in the following manner:

> The very extremely eternally immortal vampire lunged at the sullen teenager.

#

Run-on sentences are useful when transcribing the remarks of annoying people:

> So I went into this thrift shop and I saw the cutest leather jacket that looked all 1970s and patchwork and it reminded me a bit of Missoni because the colors were all blue and mustard and green and a really nice coral color and I tried it on and it fit me OK but I didn't have eight dollars to buy

> it and my friend Yves said he would lend me the money but I didn't want to take it so I put it back on the rack and went to the ATM because I didn't think anyone would buy that jacket in five minutes, you know, and then I got lunch and ate a bagel with red onion and tomato which made my breath absolutely reek but Yves had a mint, so that was good, and we went back to the store and the jacket was gone and it was oh-so-tragic and I don't know how I'll live without it but enough about me how was your day?

#

Shifting your point of view adds a sophisticated and avant-garde feeling to your writing:

> Us was walking down the street noticing that my shoes had become scuffed; you had been longtime companions, we five: my shoes, I feet and your mom.

#

The **passive voice** should be avoided by you.

#

Relative clauses are good to have so your family reunions go smoothly:

> The barbecue pit where the uncles gathered seemed slightly satanic.

#

It is all right to occasionally end a sentence with a **preposition**. However, you *never* end a sentence with a proposition:

> The mayor's statement was something the entire council could agree with, but would you like to go out to dinner with me tonight?

#

"Between" is used to refer to two items, "among" for three to ninety-nine, "centimong" for one hundred or more:

> Judges now begin the arduous task of choosing from centimong the two hundred contestants who auditioned for the baby-painting contest.

#

The **colon** can often be used to introduce a complete thought:

> There is a very easy scatological joke for the "colon" entry: This is not it.

#

When joining together double, triple, quadruple, or quintuple **prefixes**, always use a hyphen:

> sub-sub-sub-sub-sub-paragraph; non-non-non-heinous

#

If a sentence is too complex and no amount of punctuation will clarify things, it is sometimes best to simply start from scratch. "That that is is; that that is not is not" can be rewritten as *How do I know that the color blue to you is the color blue to me, man? Whoa.*

#

Brackets should not be used, as they cannot be transmitted over the wire. Instead, **use parentheses**, as news scientists finally broke that barrier in 1978. However, use parentheses sparingly. The sensuous curves may prove too lascivious for more sensitive readers.

#

Avoid overuse of **exclamation points**. Only use them in direct quotations or in articles about advertisers' really, really good appliance sales.

#

Quotation marks are commonly used to indicate sarcasm in an article: *the "Honorable" Mayor Wilson*; *the Canton Memorial Hospital for "Children."* They are also occasionally used for direct quotations.

#

Proper capitalization is key. The poet E. E. Cummings was just covering up for a severe learning disability.

#

You cannot choose relative clauses, yet you can always pick your friend clauses.

#

The first official **Subject-Verb Agreement** was signed in Geneva, Switzerland, in 1896.

#

The **present perfect tense** is always formed with "have," "has," and a nice big cup of coffee. Future perfect tense substitutes a nice big cup of digital space coffee.

#

The **irony mark** is a nonstandard punctuation symbol that resembles a backward question mark and is intended to help the reader recognize when irony is being employed. Ironically, it is only employed by writers who make their irony so obvious that a mark isn't needed in the first place or by writers who aren't quite clear on the concept of irony.

#

The **asterisk** is a punctuation symbol that looks like an asshole. Thanks a lot, Kurt Vonnegut.

VERBS

Verbs are the most important words ever. We will stab anyone who says otherwise. See? We couldn't have written that threatening sentence without the verb "stab." Verbs are important action words that people use every day, even when they are not threatening one another—yet

VERB TENSES

If your verbs are tense, send them out for a nice massage.

Present tense: Batman *is* the best.

Past tense: Superman *escaped* the destruction of his home world, Krypton.

Future tense: The Flash *won't travel* through time to kill his great-grandfather next week.

Present progressive tense: The pirate *is knitting* himself some stripy socks.

Past progressive tense: The lumberjack *was cutting* the tree down when his chainsaw slipped and bisected his torso.

Future progressive tense: Bruce Wayne *will be speaking* at a Wayne Industries board meeting on the eleventh. Batman will be strangely absent.

Present perfect: I *have* a talking boil on my shoulder that is helping to advance my career.

Past perfect: I *hadn't thought* I'd been trapped by nostalgia for the fourteenth century until I accidentally found myself crowned king at the renaissance fair.

Future perfect: By Wednesday morning I *will have created* the ultimate doomsday weapon.

many journalists are unsure of how to verb properly. Let's review how to spot verbs and then how to verb like a pro.

Instructions: Find the "action verbs" hiding like explosive devices in the following sentences.

1. Action Jackson leaped into action.
2. Momma said knock you out.
3. Dad was infected with the rage virus.
4. The Viking ate Tim.

Answers:

1. "Action," "action"
2. "said," "knock"
3. Dad, noooo!
4. Tim should have run.

NOUNS

Everybody knows what nouns are, except stupid people and monkeys. A noun is a word that names stuff. Nouns often follow words like "the," "um," and "y'know." What most people don't know is how to "noun up" a sentence real good. Nouns are your stars, so let them shine!

Instructions: Find the nouns in these sentences. For added difficulty, close your eyes while reading.

1. The meteor cracked open and Liza Minnelli emerged.
2. My son took my crack pipe without asking.

3. Go, go Godzilla!
4. That fern is reading my mind.

Answers:

1. "meteor," "Liza Minnelli"
2. "son," "pipe"
3. "oyster," "cult"
4. The fern is making me write this. It wants you to move it to a shadier spot.

ADJECTIVES

Adjectives are fancy words that affect or modify the meaning of nouns. For instance, the noun "lover" is perfectly fine as it is, but by adding an adjective like "turbo" we turn it into something wonderful: "turbo lover." Adjectives are like word magic.

Sadly, most professional writers are unaware of the existence of adjectives! Now the secret is out, thanks to us, because we're awesome. That's an adjective, son.

Instructions: Pick out the adjectives in the following sentences, if you dare!

1. Stage three of the virus turned Dad into a ravenous, murdering ghoul who pursued our terrified family dog.
2. The pirate king's eager fingers tore at the tight lacing on Edith's black silk corset as his hungry mouth clamped down on her lush, trembling lips.

3. The buxom Edith protested that her loutish husband would hear them, but he was being entertained by the lusty French maid.
4. The red dog barked at the scared boy.

Answers:

1. "ravenous," "murdering," "terrified," "family"
2. Oh, man, this is getting good.
3. That's it. . . . Here we go. . . .
4. OH, COME ON.

THE FIVE-PARAGRAPH ESSAY

Surely no childhood trauma measures up to the forced writing of the five-paragraph essay. Now we've worked hard so you don't have to. Fill in the blanks to create your own superior version of the five-paragraph essay and work through your lingering childhood issues.

First Paragraph

Hook:

This essay will ________ your mind, so sit back and ________ for the ride of your life, ________.

Thesis:

Batman is the most ________, as shown in ________, ________, and ________.

Transition:

If you don't read the next paragraph, I will ________ your ________. Remember, I know where you ________.

Second Paragraph

Supporting idea:

As shown in the great work of literature ________, Batman is more ________ than ________.

Example:

In *Superman/Batman: Saga of the Super Sons,* Batman ________ and ________ his own________.

Example:

In *Batman: The Killing Joke,* Batman ________ and ________.

Example:

In World's Finest #___, Batman ________ shit up!

Transition:

Remember what I said before about ________ your ________? That goes double if you don't read the next paragraph.

Third Paragraph

Supporting idea:

Sometimes I wish I could ________ Batman's ________ and then ________.

Example:

No, I am not ________. I just ________ Batman.

Example:

Really, you don't need to react by ________.

Example:

Fine, if you don't ________ my ________ of Batman, it is your loss.

Transition:

Is it Tuesday? I want to ________ some ________ tacos.

Concluding Paragraph

Restatement of thesis (in different words):

You must not be very intelligent if I have to say again: Batman is ________.

Summary of ideas:

I have conclusively proved that ________ Batman and Batman ________ Batman.

Call to action:

Yodel ________ ayyyyyyy ________ heeeeeeee!

FREQUENTLY CONFUSED WORDS

adapt/adept/adopt The adept writer adapted the true crime story into a screenplay after adopting the persona of Sam Spade.

allusion/illusion Overturning a table of wedding cake was an allusion to the video "November Rain" from the Guns N' Roses album *Use Your Illusion I.*

ascent/assent The unfortunate explorer made his ascent of the mountain despite lacking assent from his Sherpa guide.

assure/ensure Destro assured Cobra Commander that his weapons would ensure the complete destruction of G.I. Joe.

bare/bear Before fighting a bear bare-handed, you must learn the ancient secrets of Kyokushin karate.

bizarre/bazaar Bizarro sold bizarre toilet-paper cozies at the church bazaar.

cereal/serial The serial killer always ate bran cereal before going out on a stabbing.

device/devise MacGyver devised an incendiary device out of earwax, dryer lint, and a My Little Pony named Baby Tiddly Winks.

edition/addition Johnny Gill was a fatal addition to New Edition.

flare/flair The flares at the Misfits concert singed Stormer's keytar. Rio's purple mullet demonstrated his flair for fashion.

gorilla/guerrilla Gorilla Grodd trained a guerrilla army of telepathic gorilla soldiers, but the Flash defeated them with the power of the Speed Force.

Hardy/hearty The Hardy boys gave a hearty "hello" to their neighborhood police chief.

incite/insight Sonny Chiba incited a bear's murderous rage, but his karate insight allowed him to defeat his ursine enemy.

jam/jamb/jambon I laid a trap for the French butcher by smearing jam on the doorjamb. When he slipped, I sneaked away with a jambon.

knight/night/Knight Rider Kitt's sensors glowed red in the night as Michael Knight, better known as Knight Rider, battled a man armed with a knight's jousting lance.

lie/lay If you lie down with pastry chefs, you will wake up with fabulous layer cake.

meet/meat/Met I slipped some dried buffalo meat in my purse to prepare for my meeting with an anemic tenor at the Met.

Nome/gnome The garden gnomes of Nome, Alaska, wear Polarfleece to keep them toasty during the long winters.

GLOSSARY

ampersand Sand infused with extreme sports drink.

apostrophes Use apostrophes with care. Be aware of correct possession, as joint possession can get you a minimum five-year sentence in many states.

article There are only three of these, so be sure to use them sparingly so you don't run out. "A" and "an" are the indefinite, or "weak-ass" articles; "the" is the definite, or "King Shit of Article Town" article.

backslash The back of an extremely hairy guitarist.

caret An evil perpetuated on consumers by the diamond industry.

dash Used when there is a sudden change in thought within a sentence.

Mrs. Dash Used as a seasoning substitute when there is a sudden change in blood pressure within a sentence.

ellipsis Can be used to indicate halting speech in a direct quote. If such speech is the result of a seizure, use an epilepsis.

em space Where Dorothy's aunt lives.

grave accent A very serious accent often heard during Oscar season. See: **impactful whispering, hushed shouting.**

hyphen A gentlewoman's secret treasure.

independent clause The result of a divorce at the North Pole. See: **elf custody.**

inverted comma Medal-winning trick from the 2004 X Games.

inverted question and exclamation marks Mirror-universe punctuation discovered by Dr. Henry Pym.

parenthetical aside Additional and often personal information included in a sentence, which should never be used in a news story according to our (douchebag) copy editors.

period Ask your mother.

Solidus One of the soldiers who fought with Maximus in the Russell Crowe classic *Gladiator*.

subordinate clause "OK, if I make this shot, you have to be my slave for a week."

syntax An extremely uncomfortable pair of pants.

Tilde Ginger actress known for her unconventional lifestyle.

umlaut Punctuation reserved for the exclusive use of metal bands.

<13>

MEDIA LAW: YOU ARE SO SCREWED

Years of litigation. Millions of dollars. Your name and image dragged through the mud in the most public venues imaginable. No, you're not a Kardashian—you're a writer, and you're one of the most popular lawsuit targets in the most litigious society in human history.

And with your oversensitive and misinformed audience, it is very likely that you (yes, even you, you long-haired hippie) will need to consider the boundaries of good taste and legal liability known as *MEDIA LAW.*

While it is true no one REALLY cares what you have to say about anything, it's entirely possible that through some combination of chance, fate, and pop-cultural ephemera you could actually profit from your stupid thoughts and/or opinions. And when those dimes start to pour in, that's when the lawyers come out of the woodwork.

Face facts, Hemingway: It is unlikely your work succeeded on its own merits. So ask yourself these questions:

1) Did you knowingly steal portions of your writings?

2) Have you invaded the privacy of vacuous, annoying public figures to garner attention for your "journalism"?

3) Have you unwittingly become the whipping boy of the Church of Scientology because you once wrote an article about how Tom Cruise is "kinda gayish" (your words, not mine)?

Congratulations, you could get sued! And what a marvelous ride it will be. Motions! Subpoenas! Judges! Juries! Bailiffs! Oh, the friends you'll make in jail!

If you want to survive, in both the professional and the literal not-dying sense, you'll have to learn what's cool and what's totally uncool in the world of media law. Most lawyers charge by the hour, but we offer a lifetime of knowledge for one low, extremely reasonable price. Learn how to skate the thin line of legality, and perpetuate the great American dream of succeeding on ethically questionable practices as you laugh all the way to the bank.

Note: The following chapter does not constitute actual legal advice. What are we, lawyers?*

*One of us actually is a lawyer, but he hates his job and would sell you out for half a Marlboro and a Flavor Flav B-side.

THE BASICS

Because writers are better than normal people, they have certain privileges that protect them from libel claims. It's pretty great. But just in case you're caught walking around some restricted area with pockets full of cash, you'd better know just what those privileges are.

Little known fact: anything's OK as long as you preface it with **"In my opinion."** No, really, you could write that the earth is hexagonal, and as long as you made it clear that that's your opinion, it is totally your right to do it.

The phrase **"in all fairness"** is also protected under privilege. As long as you say, "In all fairness," it's totally cool if you publish a comment like "Senator Maxwell believes the earth is hexagonal, which in all fairness makes him the stupidest stupid person to ever say a stupid, stupid thing."

Though it shares the word "fair" with the above privilege, **"fair report"** is more about the reporting than about the fairness. It means everything's fine as long as you fairly report on what's going on. So if you're caught with the aforementioned wads of cash, just write about it accurately later on and you should be in the clear: "Yeah, I stole a bunch of money. Come and get me, bitches!"

#

As a writer, it's important that you do all you can to remain **impartial and disinterested**. This means not having opinions. About anything! Or at the very least not putting them on display. Here are some things to avoid:

- political signs or stickers
- voting or paying taxes
- attending rallies, fund-raisers, or political ritual murders
- serving on the board of a charity or otherwise helping the less fortunate
- investing in companies, thereby showing partiality to one company over another
- purchasing products or services from those companies
- going to church or otherwise showing partiality to one god over another
- showing love or concern for anyone

#

Like it or not, the Supreme Court decided years ago that it's not OK to just go around bursting into people's houses and writing about the strange religious rituals and sex practices going on in there. Worse yet, the **right to privacy** extends beyond simple home invasions. Even writing about stuff you don't need a telephoto lens to see can piss people off! Keep in mind that doing any of these things could land you in privacy jail:

"Misappropriation" is taking someone's likeness or image and using it to sell a product for promotional purposes, like when Bob Dylan was in that Victoria's Secret commerci—Wait, he did that on purpose? Man!

"Public disclosure" is when something about someone is disclosed to the public. This can be something like where the person lives or how tall he or she is. "Public disclosure" will be discussed in greater detail in this book's companion volume, *Write More Good: After Dark.*

"Intrusion" is entering into a person's personal space, such as his or her home, into his or her private interests, or, most diabolically of all, *his or her very mind*.

"False light" is showing someone in a light that is totally bogus and dumb, like a black light. Weak.

CASE STUDY: 2 LIVE CREW

Copyright law in the United States is pretty stupid. It says that you're basically not allowed to use others' creative works for personal profit. See? Totally stupid.

But there is one way to escape copyright infringement liability: through the legal doctrine of fair use.

The U.S. Supreme Court, in the case of *Campbell v. Acuff-Rose Music, Inc.*, 510 U.S. 569 (1994), held that the commercial nature of a parody does not render it a presumptively unfair use of copyrighted material. Rather, a parody's commercial character is only one element to be weighed in a fair-use inquiry. When the members of 2 Live Crew released the song "Pretty Woman," based on the Roy Orbison rock ballad "Oh, Pretty Woman," Orbison's production company, Acuff-Rose Music, Inc., refused to grant a license to the group. The group released the song anyway and sold over a million copies of the recording. Acuff-Rose brought suit for copyright infringement, and the Supreme Court ruled in favor of Luther Campbell and 2 Live Crew, forever preserving porn companies' right to make movies with titles such as *Ally McSqueal, Choke-a-hontas,* and *Chinny Chinny Gang Bang.*

There will be other times for jokes, for humorous tips, and for snarky comments. But for the moment, the authors of *Write More Good* salute you, Luke, DJ Mr. Mixx, Fresh Kid Ice, Amazing, and Brother Marquis. May you forever be "as nasty as you wanna be."

It is inappropriate in any circumstance to **accept a gift from a source**, even something as small as a bottle of water. It seems harmless, but what if you discover the very source you accepted the water from is, in fact, the world's most famous water thief? And then you tell him or her that you're going to blow this story wide open, and he or she tells you: "Remember that bottle of water I gave you? I'll tell them all. I'll tell everyone." You'd be ruined. Ruined! You say that sounds unlikely? That it could never happen? Ask a friend of ours. His name? JAYSON BLAIR.

#

Plagiarism. It's a big problem. It's also one of the building blocks of modern journalism. But with Internets and Googles and all that, it's easier to catch than ever. You gotta be careful, man! Get creative with your pinching! Here's a handy guide for how to use other people's stuff without being branded as a nasty, filthy, dirty plagiarizer:

- ORIGINAL SENTENCE: *Mayor Rex Wasserman was caught with his hand in the proverbial cookie jar this week, as he was found to have been funneling city contract money into his own private business interests.*

- PLAGIARISM: *Found funneling city contract money into his own private business interests, Mayor Rex Wasserman has been caught with his hand in the proverbial cookie jar.*

- NOT PLAGIARISM: *Mayor Rex Wasserman smashed the piggy bank with a hammer, so to speak, this week when I, the reporter writing this very story, discovered that he was snatching up city contracts for his own shit.*

- REALLY NOT PLAGIARISM: *Major Rich Wagerman funneled a whole bunch of cookies this week while he is supposed to be dieting, so his wife was probably really mad, but why was she interested? It was none of her business.*

#

There are many ways to harm others through your writing. Many people see completely false and malicious statements both online and off as "unwarranted" or "unnecessary" or "illegal" or "actionable." If you plan to write about public and private figures, be aware of the following **claims for defamation** and ways you can work around such claims with some easy editing techniques:

Slander is a form of defamation where one speaks false and malicious claims meant to damage someone's character or reputation.

- BAD: *Did you hear Ken Lowery, cocreator of* Write More Good, *has a blazing case of herpes?*

- SOLUTION: Remain coy; assert nothing, but deny nothing.

- BETTER SOLUTION: *I'm not saying that Ken Lowery, cocreator of* Write More Good, *has a blazing case of herpes. But I'm not saying he* doesn't.

Libel is a form of defamation where one communicates, especially in writing, false and malicious claims meant to damage someone's character or reputation.

- BAD: *Ken Lowery, cocreator of* Write More Good, *has a blazing case of herpes.*
- SOLUTION: Hide your claim in clever code.
- BETTER SOLUTION: *Ken Lowery may or may not have a certain disease that rhymes with shmerpes. And if he* did, *it would be blazing.*

AVOIDING LIBEL

The following words, among others, may be considered grounds for a libel suit if used in a story to refer to a specific individual:

bad	coward	rapist
niggardly	jerk-ass	Bureau Chief
Nazi	Glenn Beck	Sherlockian
shyster	goober	fwesp
funtastic	vase	jive turkey
unethical	soylent	Democrat

Hearsay is a statement made outside of court, usually based on secondhand knowledge.

- BAD: *I heard Ken Lowery, cocreator of* Write More Good, *has a blazing case of herpes.*

- SOLUTION: Blame it on someone!
- BETTER SOLUTION: *Mark Hale told me Ken Lowery has a blazing case of herpes. What a dick move, right? But good to know.*

HANDLING YOURSELF IN COURT

It happens to the best of us. Something you've written for publication has gotten you sued, and now you're in front of a judge. During this proceeding you will be forced to behave in accordance with a set of rules; breaking these rules can lead to the judge holding you in contempt of court. This is not a desirable outcome. Here are some guidelines to help gauge whether you are in danger of being held in contempt.

1) The judge no longer thinks your *Ernest Goes to Jail* impressions are relevant and/or humorous. The judge is wrong, but that's beside the point.

2) You incessantly quote . . . *And Justice For All*, rendering your throat completely raw. It's best to save this for when someone in court is actually "out of order."

3) You have yelled "Objection!" three times in a row, followed by a fist pump and an attempted high five to your attorney when your own witness is on the stand. This could be seen as excessive.

4) You have misappropriated the judge's gavel and attempted to start a chant of "We will rock you" in the courtroom. No matter how well the audience responds, cease immediately.

LANDMARK CASES IN U.S. PRESS LAW

New York Times v. *Sullivan* SCOTUS! ruled that public officials must prove "actual malice" to recover damages in defamation suits. In other words, you can call the mayor a sheep fucker so long as you're really nice about it and invite him over for lamb chops afterward.

Associated Press v. Walker In which SCOTUS! extended the protections of NYT *v. Sullivan* to public figures. Swap out "Tom Cruise" for "mayor" in the above example.

Roe v. Wade Saved the collective bacon of a lot of traveling reporters, I tell you what.

If these guidelines fail you and you find yourself handcuffed and heading toward jail, remain calm. Begin yelling "Attica!" repeatedly in hopes of inciting a riot. Then fake your own death—even going so far as to kill and mutilate another inmate who sort of resembles you—and escape.

#

The rich and powerful will often use the threat of a lawsuit to discourage reporters from investigating things they'd rather not have investigated. This is known as a **"chilling effect"** or "dick move." The best way to counteract the dick move is to fabricate all your stories and sources. It's common sense that fictional people don't sue. Also, fictional people fight Russian spies and bed more sexy Martian princesses than real people do, which will give your police-blotter stories that extra pop they might otherwise lack.

GLOSSARY

absolute privilege Enjoyed by the inhabitants of Cape Cod, Hyannis Port, and Bill Gates's orbiting space fortress.

burden of proof The theory that proof must bring civilized society to the savages.

closed meetings Meetings where public officials discuss "legal issues," such as how they're all going to vote on something and how much they hate the press.

common-law malice Happens in most marriages after seven to ten years.

defamation 1. Public statements or communications regarding an individual, business, or product that portray the subject in a negative light: *Anything done by Amy Winehouse defames the country of Great Britain.* 2. What happened to that guy who played Epstein on *Welcome Back, Kotter* and that other one from that movie, name's on the tip of my tongue. See: **DeWitt, Joyce.**

dicta Legal term used by judges in opinions for the sole purpose of giggling behind chamber doors.

ethics Things that really good writers don't have to worry about.

fair comment *The deaths of Hicks and Newt in* Alien^3 *really undercut my enjoyment of* Aliens *upon repeat viewings.*

fault What a plaintiff must prove in a libel suit or a dispute over who broke Dad's favorite lamp.

First Amendment Still exists.

gag order 1. Fifty dollars extra per hour, but she might cut you a deal if you pay up front. 2. Avoid the creamed chipped beef. That's all we're saying.

Government in the Sunshine Act A 1976 law to make those pasty white senators look less horrifying to the public. Also known as "Congressional Field Day."

harm or injury What people want to do to you after you libel them.

intellectual property Laws involving ownership of brains between zombies.

liable/libel Writers are *liable* to live the rest of their lives in a refrigerator box behind the A&P if they lose a *libel* suit.

negligence [WILL FINISH LATER]

open meeting Meeting to which journalists are invited and at which no real government work gets done.

plagiarism Use or imitation of the language or written works of another author, conveyed as the author's own work. Now legalized due to Wikipedia.

Private Figure Nickname most lawyers give their genitals.

public document Information that is available to every citizen and will take you two months to obtain.

public figure 1. A person you cannot avoid no matter how hard you try. 2. That hot chick across the courtyard who likes to go topless with the blinds open.

publicity What you give public figures every day, but sometimes they get mad about it.

published Not read.

quash To set aside or void. Add "S" for delicious soups.

slander Distinct from libel in that it is spoken rather than written. Much more difficult to prove in court, so burn your notes before you call the mayor a sheep fucker.

state shield laws Laws protecting reporters from the violent, dangerous, and corrupt practices of Michael Chiklis's rogue police character. See: **state commish laws.**

temporary restraining order See: **paparazzi.**

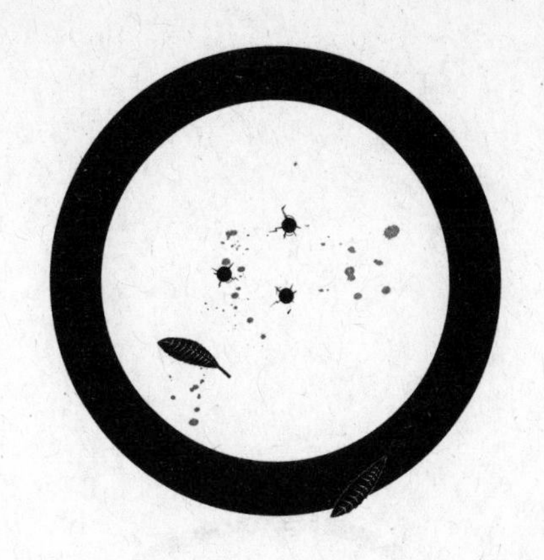

<14>

THE MORGUE:

THE DEAD

LIVE!

PRINT
MEDIA

Language is a mutable, evolving thing, and any guide to it will be more a map of the terrain than a blueprint.

Chaucer's English is barely recognizable to modern speakers (which is a pity, since they'd otherwise appreciate his hilarious fart jokes) and, as the science-fiction show *Firefly* theorized, in the future we will speak a combination of Chinese and Cowboy, but only for half a season.

From the earliest days of the written word there arose a need for it to convey meaning in a precise and correct manner. One need only look at the famous Bent Pyramid to see the disastrous consequences of writing a falcon head when you meant to use a lotus leaf. And had there been a group of "bureau high priests" in ancient Sumeria, the royal scribes might not have violated the "II before < except after I =" rule so often.

When paper developed, writing became more commonplace (would you doodle as much if it meant having to fire clay tablets or carve rock?) and the Chinese and the Romans had a contest to see who could make their language more ridiculously complicated. When it was discovered that Rome's numerical system rendered "59 509" as "LIX DIX," Rome won. Because that's hilarious.

In the Middle Ages, the need for precise and accurate language became paramount. Only one book was being written, but since it was the Bible, getting it right was key. Monks toiled ceaselessly to copy the word of God by hand, and believe me, that is one Editor you don't want to piss off.

Unfortunately, God's attention got diverted during the Siege of Jerusalem and a few errors crept in that have only recently been caught. Lazarus, whom Jesus is said to have raised from the dead, was actually named Jazzarus, and there is evidence he was a robot that transformed into a car. In addition, modern biblical scholars believe that "Do this in memory of me" was originally "Do this in memory of Meat Loaf," but both the dish and the popular singer were still two millennia away, so the disciples didn't catch the reference.

With the development of the printing press, not only could text be mass-produced quickly, it could also be mass-produced quickly and incorrectly. Publishers now had the ability to distribute baseless lies and rumors written in barely recognizable English at a rate that would remain unmatched until the invention of YouTube comments. Something needed to be done, and thus the "editor" was invented by Galileo in 1604.

The Age of Enlightenment further put text into the hands of regular people, culminating with the invention of the ultimate medium for human expression, the newspaper. The role of editor was perfected by Benjamin Franklin, and several people tried to wrangle spelling and grammar into codified rules to make communication easier. At last the common man found himself in a realm where only priests and kings had walked before. The hoi polloi took to the printed word with an enthusiasm that held until television destroyed it in the 1950s.

Nothing further of any consequence happened until

the invention of the Internet by America Online in September 1993.

It's easy to see, then, that what was relevant in the past may no longer be relevant in the present, especially when new technology changes the landscape of the language, such as when killer robots travel back in time to destroy the mother of their nemesis. Anyone trying to make sense of the ridiculous gibberish we call the English language needs to be able to change with the times, and this stylebook is no exception.

Here, then, are some entries from previous editions. At one time, journalists risked being fired for not knowing these guidelines. Their careers ended and their ability to obtain food and shelter threatened, they resorted to painful methods of prematurely ending their lives that left their pitiful remains to be identified solely through dental records or spiritualists. These days, we can just laugh at this trivial bullshit.

THE GHOST OF BASICS PAST

"Big Bang" is sufficient; descriptions such as "Biggest Bang Ever," "That Was a Huge Fuckin' Bang," and "The Bang to End All Bangs" assume future bangs won't be even larger, so let's hold off and see what comes along before committing ourselves. (13,700,000,000 BC)

#

All stories regarding the extinction of dinosaurs shall be covered as a natural disaster occurring via meteorites and volcanoes. No one shall know the true cause of the extinction of the dinosaurs: socialism. (65,000,000 BC)

#

Articles on climate change are old hat; there is little to no supporting evidence that this alleged forthcoming "ice age" is imminent, and running such fearmongering articles is irresponsible, especially considering how hot it was last summer. (70,000 BC)

#

No make reference to fanciful concepts like "fire" or "wheel" or you are banished from cave. (50,000 BC)

#

Do not put Adam's most recent animal naming on the front page, as this is no longer considered "newsworthy." (4000 BC)

#

Always knead your clay carefully and shape it into a tablet before noting down the crop records with your stylus. (3000 BC)

#

Downplay the involvement of extraterrestrials in pyramid construction. Pharaoh would be displeased if his outsourcing of contracts to non-Egyptians were revealed. (2519 BC)

#

Despite the helpful suggestion of King Odysseus, the correct way to describe a long and eventful trip is still just "a long and eventful trip." (1184 BC)

#

In stories about severe weather, always include the names, addresses, and actions of all those responsible for angering Zeus so badly. (477 BC)

#

It is no longer necessary to cover developments in warfare due to the invincible nature of the Macedonian phalanx and their deadly sarissas. Just assume that Macedonia will win and adjust your articles accordingly. (322 BC)

#

Good wall, Ch'in Shih Huang Ti? We'd go so far as to call it great! (206 BC)

#

"Jesus of Nazareth" on first reference. On subsequent references, "Jesus," "Jesus Christ," and known alias "Rex Honeybone" are acceptable. (AD 28)

#

All Norse communication must include the phrase "slaughter Anglo-Saxons in their mead hall until their blood flows as freely as the water in the North Sea." (1055)

#

For future reference, all instances of "shit," "fuck," and "cunt" shall be changed to "merde," "baiser," and "King William of Normandy," respectively. (1066)

THE ONGOING DEATH OF PRINT JOURNALISM

Radio will destroy print journalism. (1930)
Television will destroy print journalism. (1948)
The Internet will destroy print journalism. (2001)
The invasion of the lizard-bots from beyond hyperspace will destroy print journalism. (2110)

#

The moderne fadde aemoungste the younge of writing wordes thhe saemme waye eache tim theye are rittenne isse a siggne of tehe degennerennceye offe thee ayge annde shulde notte be encoraggedde. (1200)

> Whan that Aprille, with hise shoures soote,
> The droghte of March hath perced to the roote,
> And bathed every veyne in swich licour,
> Of which vertu engendred is the flour;
> Thane shalle ye runne thine "Stormewatche" oupdatte.
> (1390)

#

Referring to the current unpleasantness as the "Ten Years' War" is unnecessarily negative. Please try to keep stories on current events upbeat. (1347)

#

When penning a missive concerning the Black Death, wear a garland of rose petals, lest you accidentally summon a plague spirit with your quill. (1348)

#

No more stories about all these fake "shrouds" going around. Those hucksters in Turin don't need any more publicity. (1380)

#

Now that this Gutenberg cat has invented the printing press, you can no longer blame your errors on other folks' poor transcribing. Make sure you've got your facts straight! (We'll work on consistent spelling later.) (1450)

#

We will no longer accept for publication letters to the editor that have been nailed to our office doors. Spend the guilder to have a messenger deliver it. (1517)

#

When referring to the wife of His Royal Highness King Henry VIII, leave the space for the name blank until the last minute, just in case. (1524)

#

Best ye avoyde yon twice-told Negative, in the manner of "shall not not," lest ye sow Muche Confusion and be deemst thus a Wytche, and be burned thus upon the stake unto thy death; or else shall ye be named Campaigne Strategist for a major politickal Candidate, and in God's Own time be burned thus upon the stake unto thy death. (1550)

HOW TO WRITE ABOUT YOUR FAIR MISTRESS (1597)

"O fie and rue," the hapless authors cry
Whilst penning verse to a young lady.
Shall I compare full lips or blazing eye
To glints of sun or something shady?

With poems one must carefully compose.
Be not florid, lewd, vulgar, or perverse.
E'en whilst mentioning reverse cowgirl pose,
Speak of your lady's bits as fair in verse.

All poets write of bosoms, eyes, and hair,
Yet easy similes sometimes rankle.
Take pen in hand for your Lady's derriere
And sing of her fibula or right ankle.

Follow Cupid's tips for written romance
And with luck, with wile, get into her pants.

#

It is never appropriate to use "Elizaleigh," "Ralizabeth," or "Sir Waltizabeth Ralegis" when reporting on Her Royal Highness's impending marriage. (1563)

#

In reference to the author William Shakespeare, lately of the venerable Globe Theatre, "the Bard" is acceptable upon second reference, as are "Christopher Marlowe" and "Edward de Vere," as both are widely known noms de plume of the former. (1603)

#

Following an informative visit by the agents of the Inquisition, the editors would like to retract our previous and grossly incorrect statements that the earth revolved around the sun. (1633)

#

All women accused of witchcraft are to be presumed guilty until proven guilty. Or dead. But still guilty. (1692)

#

Dr. Johnson can take his *Dictionary of the English Language* and shove it up his ass. (1755)

#

Avoid confusing the Stamp Act and the Tea Act, as doing so could interfere with the King's plans for the Tea and Stamp Act, the Tea Acting Stamp Act, and the Stamping Tea Act. (1773)

#

Despite all the rumors you might hear to the contrary, Benjamin Franklin should not be referred to as a "man whore." (1776)

#

All Good Writers and Typesetters will consider the Appearance of their Words and Phrases and capitalize accordingly, bringing the Best Emphasis to those Phrases that seem the most Important. (1797)

#

Refer to the Sedition Act by its full title, "The Finest Law Ever Written by Man in Any Form or Fashion, Dear God Don't Put Us in Jail." (1798)

#

To get the best work out of your scriveners, shackle them to their desks and water them daily. Exposure to sunlight may cause them to wilt, but a tiny bit of stale bread and a thimble of ale administered every four hours may revive them. (1852)

#

It is inappropriate to use the term "Dickensian" as an insult in your literary headlines. (1855)

#

Some of our more sensitive readers in the Confederate states may not like our using the term "Civil War." Publications in those areas may prefer to use these alternative names for the War Between the States:

- The War of Northern Meanness for No Apparent Good Reason We Can See
- The Conflict of Just Leave Us Alone
- Secession for Success!
- The War That People Say Is All About Slavery But There Are So Many Other Causes (1862)

SEXUAL SCANDAL THROUGHOUT HISTORY

No matter how well known they be, the proclivities of Mr. Jefferson as regards his slaves are best left unprinted, lest we besmirch the name of a fine American. Remember, editors: He's the PRESIDENT. (1802)

No one is interested in hearing about the president's personal sexual preference. We, the esteemed media, have more important things to focus on here. I mean, come on guys, have some self-respect. He's the PRESIDENT. (1863)

So this lady sang "Happy Birthday" to the president. It's his business who he spends time with. We're the media; it's our duty to cover more important things. I mean, of course the guy gets some play. He's the PRESIDENT! (1962)

Guys, people REALLY care about whether our president got a blow job from some chick. It's our DUTY as the media to cover this. I mean, he's the PRESIDENT! (1997)

#

"Mammy," not "Mommy." Also, "Mam" is acceptable, as that is three-fifths of the full word. (1863)

#

Moving pictures are simply too fast to write about. Just give it up, fellows. (1867)

#

Don't call redskins "Buffalo Botherers." Y'all don't want to get letters from uppity Quaker types back east. (1870)

#

When writin' up the exploits of the outlaws and gunslingers that have captured the imaginations of those pantywaists back east, ya have to give them an appropriate frontier name. Because that's what those tenderfoots expect 'cause of those damn dime novels they keep readin'. The method is, take the Christian name of that varmint and add one of the following either before or after: Two-Gun, Colt, Bandito, Rawhide, Trigger, Western, All-Star, Apache, Bronco, Buckskin, Wild, Forty-Five, Deadeye, Hopalong, Outlaw, Little, Frito, Mask, Injun, Tex, Okie, or Hex. If the Christian name is known only to the outlaw and God, just take two of them there words and mash 'em together into something that would sound suitably menacing for an eastern tea drinker. (1890)

#

TYPESETTERS: Occasionally, in your paper's basement smelting house and type foundry, a mistake will be made in the process of melting down the steel and casting the letterforms you need for that day's edition. Bring any imperfections to the attention of your editor, who will make sure the offending orphan's bread portion is withheld that day. (1898)

#

PICTURES SELL PAPERS. So when in need of predeath portraits of victims of trolley accidents, glue-vat drownings, subway train cave-ins, et cetera, a good resource is the homes of next of kin. If they are not willing to provide a photogravure or painting for reproduction, try posing as one of the following to gain entry into the home: milkman, constable, gaslight repairman, provisions salesman, carpet sweep. (1906)

#

When preparing photographic or artistic renderings of the kaiser, have the paste-up man add devil's horns. (1915)

#

Until the treacherous Huns have been defeated, refer to German shepherds as "Alsatians," hamburgers as "victory steaks," and frankfurters as "lips-and-ass sausages." (1917)

#

When surreptitiously taking photos of a man during a hanging, be sure to smuggle the camera apparatus under a false hunchback, with the shutter control concealed along your left trouser leg. (1919)

#

All right youse mugs, listen up. Now that the boys and me are in charge of this here "stylebook," there's going to be some changes, unless you want to see your pretty little faces messed up. First of all, all these "mafia" stories you keep running. There ain't no such thing as a mafia. Any time you run a story about this so-called mafia, remember that you are defaming the good name of patriotic Italian businessmen. And remember that Fabrizzio's Butcher and DiMarchino's Concrete are your biggest advertisers at the moment. Second of all, there ain't nothing wrong with no bathtub gin, and those stories of people who drink it going blind are just the feds trying to turn the public against honest Italian businessmen. Third of all, we're going to be needing some union dues from all of youse starting right about now. Don't mess up too bad and we won't have to make it, whatchucallit, "retroactive." (1921)

#

When painting slogans on your jalopy before the big game, you must include a minimum of two "23 skiddoos," three "Whoopees," four "bees knees," and an instruction for women to get out of your dreams and into your struggle buggy. (1923)

#

Given our great respect for our president and his nickname, "Silent Cal," always quote President Coolidge as simply saying, ". . ." (1923)

#

There is no need to express caution to readers of your business pages over the speculative trading currently going on within investment firms, nor should large loans be discouraged if the purpose is to invest heavily in stocks with that borrowed money. With the firm hand of a cautious Republican like President Hoover leading the nation, there is no reason to suppose that the record highs in the current market will ever diminish. (September 1929)

#

Do not use periods when referring to the pesticide/delicious food additive DDT. (1941)

#

Loose lips sink ships, so convey the arrival and departure of troop transports though broad pantomime. (1942)

#

Shit, sorry about that Harry . . . er, President Truman. (November 3, 1948, revision)

#

"Johnny B. Goode" was originally performed by an unknown white high-school student before it was stolen and popularized by Chuck Berry. This is a revision from the 1985 edition. (1955)

#

LOS ANGELES, 1950

For the benefit of those recently assigned to our Hollywood bureau, there are certain catchwords you need to use in order for your stories to conform to the house style for film industry news. Since many of these terms will be unfamiliar to you, here is a short glossary of phrases to be used in your coverage of the studios and what they mean in plain English.

- suspected communist: out homosexual
- confirmed communist: voted to form actors' union
- suspected homosexual: probable communist
- exciting new starlet: sleeps with producers
- young lady destined to go far: sleeps with reporters
- leading man material: sleeps with producers
- took a short vacation: sleeping off a drug binge
- exhaustion: being treated for alcohol poisoning
- producer: Jew

A perennial favorite for February articles is a list of the most eligible bachelors in the nation. Particularly popular subjects for these articles are Liberace, Rock Hudson, Tab Hunter, and FBI director J. Edgar Hoover and his good friend Roy Cohn. (1960)

#

War is good for some things, despite Edwin Starr's assertions. (1969)

#

"Bad mother" is an unacceptably vulgar synonym for "tough guy." Shut yo' mouth. Exception: if you talkin' 'bout Shaft, we can dig it. (1971)

#

Many of you have been phoning us asking for a generic name that can be applied to political scandals. After much discussion, we feel that the best solution is to simply apply half of the word associated with perhaps the most famous political scandal of the twentieth century, "Watergate." Example: "Water-Scam," "Water-Theft," "Water-Clash," "Water-Water," etc. (1975)

#

"Decorative utensil wear" is preferred to "coke spoon necklace" when describing celebrity fashion choices. (1976)

#

It is libel and heresy to write an article asserting that video killed the radio star. (1980)

#

The World Wide Web or Internet (colloq. "'Net"), is an alien world where computer programs written in BASIC and FORTRAN can interact as sentient humanoids in glowing neon armor with total, unrestricted access to anything you have ever typed into any computer, as well to most household appliances. They require regular ritual sacrifice and possibly a training montage set to a power ballad. Most enjoy electronic music, motorcycle racing, and the newfound expression of what you hu-mons call "love." They will die if not fed a weekly diet of brine shrimp. (1981)

#

We have always been at war with Eastasia. (1984)

#

So, like, I was preparing our new edition of the stylebook? And I looked over and noticed that Bobby? Was totally working on the business guide and using the word "Gekko-ize" every other paragraph? And I was like, "Bobby, you know that even though you may think Gordon Gekko is the bomb, it doesn't mean it is brill to use some bogus word in your writing advice." And Bobby? He said, "Bite me, bitch, you be buggin'." And I said, "Step off, Bobby!?" He is such a waste-oid. (1987)

#

Always capitalize the following timeless dances: the Macarena, the Tootsie Roll, the Cabbage Patch. (1995)

#

Stories about Iraq's stockpiling of yellowcake should not be featured in the food and culture sections unless specifically referring to Abdullah Ahad's famous indigenous dish, Iraqi Yellow Cake. If featuring this recipe, we advise you to run your feature sooner rather than later. (2003)

#

Use "unstoppable," "never-ending," or "permanent" to describe the real-estate boom. (2007)

GLOSSARY

bitch A very desirable woman indeed or a dog, which may also be desirable. (1330)

Bona to vada, I'm omi-palone for your basket According to our British offices, a polite slang phrase for discouraging the advances of a queer. (1950)

Canada Soon to be admitted as the forty-ninth state of the United States, pending legislation. (1952)

cocaine Magic "stay up late to finish laying out the front page" powder. A journalist's best friend. (1981)

comic books Colorful pulp magazines featuring the unbelievable adventures of outlandish characters. While currently fashionable, we predict that the fad will die down shortly after the troubles in Europe conclude, briefly resurge in popularity thirty years from now, and again twenty years after that, before entering a long, slow period of irrevocable decline and irrelevancy. Best not to cover them unless you have some column inches you can't sell ad space for. (1934)

commie Used to refer to anyone you want, honestly. (1953)

die hard *Never* to be used unless referring to this awesome movie. Did you see it? He was all jumping off the building, and Alan Rickman was all, "Noooo!" Man. Yeah, just say "uncompromising" or "immovable" instead. (1988)

eat my shorts An obscure and secret sexual practice of J. Edgar Hoover. (1956)

Funk Isaac Kaufmann Funk founded the company that published the *Funk & Wagnalls Standard Encyclopedia* and other reference books essential to a writer's trade. He was also the original Starchild, capable of getting his groove on in all six extraterrestrial dimensions, beating Adam Wagnalls in a game of interplanetary funksmanship when he sailed his UFO directly into the Bermuda Triangle. Can you dig it? (1894)

gadzooks Exclamation used upon a surprising sighting of a flock of zooks. As zooks do not exist, "gadzooks" should never be used. (1654)

gay bar A drinking establishment characterized by the unusual jollity of the patrons. This is probably due to the lack of women and the carefully darkened back rooms. (1900)

Gearhead An amazing automaton built by John Joseph Merlin. (1758)

geek Circus performer who bites the heads off of live animals while discussing his H. G. Wells fanfic in excruciating detail. (1907)

going postal Taking a package to the post office. (1991)

gold digger A person who digs for gold. "I'm not saying Samuel McGillicuddy is a gold digger, but he went to California with a mule and a tent and came back with a bad case of scurvy." (1849)

groovy Having the nature of being grooved; primarily used in woodworking. (1948)

HTML Home Tantalizing Meat Larder, a popular new item sold by the Clawson Refrigeration Company allowing for the home storage of cured meats. (1895)

hugger-mugger Use only to describe actions performed in secret, and not to describe the notorious Jacob Walsingham, the Overly Affectionate Bandit. (1603)

humorist Someone who is or the act of being prejudiced against one of the four humors (often yellow bile) for no good reason. (372 BC)

humorist Someone who makes piercing observations about how in Soviet Russia, one thing does the opposite thing to YOU! (1987)

law Basically just killing people. (620 BC)

Middle Ages Approximately AD 124 to AD 201. (476)

modern medicine See: **alcohol, leeches, amputation.** (1487 AD)

MP3 Family nickname for Morgan Pierce III, jet-setting playboy, heir to the Pierce Aviation fortune, and suspect in a series of cunning cat burglaries along the French Riviera. Allowable in quotes from family members, friends, or Pierce's famed defense attorney, J. Bigelow Hatsworth. (1958)

nice 1. Insulting term meaning "stupid" or "foolish"; should be used sparingly: *That person is nice.* (1288) 2. Degrading term meaning "wanton" or "licentious"; should be used only to describe the slatternly: *That person is nice.* (1389) 3. Term used to describe the coy or shy; should be used only to describe those who avoid attention: *That person is nice.* (1599) 4. Flattering term used to describe something agreeable or pleasant: *That person is nice.* (1819) 5. All-purpose term used to describe something when you can't think of anything else to say: *That person is nice.* (1902)

N.W.A. Always abbreviate. No, really. ALWAYS abbreviate. (1991)

odds bodkins Exclamation; should be used only in reaction to groups of items that can't be evenly divided by two; otherwise, use "evens bodkins." (1742)

Oedipus Complex A new shopping and entertainment district constructed at the behest of the king of

Thebes. References to his wife as a "cougar" are to be discouraged. (475 BC)

omen Pretty much the best proof we can find for shit right now. (1160)

passenger pigeon A species of wild, migratory bird that provides a cheap, inexhaustible source of food for slaves and hoboes. See: **unicorn.** (1847)

Psyche 1. Beloved of Cupid. (1400 BCE) 2. Trickery. (1971)

psyched Excited. (1983)

quaint It is highly offensive to use this term for a part of the female anatomy. Instead, replace it with the more acceptable euphemism "the 'Q' word." (1660)

queer street Slang term referring to financial trouble or shady dealings of some kind, probably derived from "Carey Street," the location of London's bankruptcy court. Never to be used in reference to Oscar Wilde's home address, as he is quite litigious about such matters. (1890)

rad A unit of measurement for the amount of radiation absorbed. Extremely radioactive things may be described as "totally rad." (1976)

royal assload The amount of material that can fit within a king's ass. Exact quantity specified by this measurement varies from reign to reign; please consult with His Royal Highness's secretary of weights and measures for details as needed. (1527)

Salieri, Antonio Still exists. (1787)

science Fringe belief system that runs counter to the proven fields of astrology and alchemy. Should not be taken seriously, but token quotes from these upstart "natural philosophers" may be used in the interest of balance. (1622)

sound barrier WARNING: NEVER TO BE MENTIONED. The theoretical barrier broken by pilot Chuck Yeager, opening a rift into the hellish fifty-third dimension, unleashing such horror as the world has never seen, which was only beaten back by the combined armies of eight nations. The mere reminder of this incident in the public's imagination could be enough to open the thin reality membrane once more, according to government scientists. (1949)

Stonewall 1. Acceptable on second reference for the infamous General Thomas J. Jackson of the damned Confederacy, whose steadfast courage and full, lush beard have nevertheless won our grudging admiration and respect. (1861) 2. Acceptable on second reference for the inn or the riots perpetrated there by those filthy queers, whose steadfast courage and smooth, chiseled jawlines have nevertheless awakened feelings in ourselves we'd rather not have to acknowledge to our spouses. (1969)

tell a vision What you do after you see your dead father's ghost and he starts getting all up in your face. (1599)

time zones Determined at the start of each week by a representative of the Vanderbilt family. You will receive a wire from the railroad notifying you as to which time zone your city is set to follow this week. (1869)

Visigoths A barbarian tribe clad all in black, distinguished by their peculiarly mournful chants when they go berserk. (476)

vomitorium This term is beginning to be seen as distasteful and offensive by the public at large. Use instead "pukeatoria." (32 BC)

war Peace. See: **ignorance (strength).** (1984; 2003)
Which A foule determiner inne leauge withe the Unholie One. The pronoune forme is acceptable. (1690)
yar 1. Standard Caribbean pirate greeting, e.g., "Yar, prepare to hoist anchor, matey! (1735) 2. Least popular *Star Trek: The Next Generation* character, e.g., "Yar: took long enough to kill her off, matey!" (1988)

CREATED AND EDITED BY

Mark Hale & Ken Lowery

THE BUREAU CHIEFS ARE

Eugene Ahn
Benjamin Birdie
David Campbell
Kevin Church
John DiBello
Josh Krach
Andrew Kunka, PhD
Dave Lartigue
Anna Neatrour
Chris Sims
Mike Sterling
Andrew Otis Weiss
RJ White
Matt Wilson
Dorian Wright